Picture-Tube Imperialism?

Picture-Tube Imperialism?

The Impact of U.S. Television on Latin America

Alan Wells

134099

ORBIS BOOKS, Maryknoll, New York

To my parents, James E. and Winifred G. Wells, and for those who know the modern world but cannot enter.

ACKNOWLEDGEMENTS

My initial interest in development was in large part the result of encounters with Professor Guenther Roth of the University of California. It was further nourished by Professor Irving L. Horowitz at Washington University. His influence on my thinking in the first part of this work far exceeds the citations to him.

Professor Nicholas J. Demerath offered his careful criticism on three earlier drafts and Professors David B. Carpenter and David Felix have each given encouragement for this work and made significant contributions to the development of its thesis. Together they composed the committee for my doctoral dissertation entitled *Development, Consumerism and Television in Latin America* (Washington University, St. Louis, May, 1970), which forms the basis for this book. They are not, of course, responsible for any remaining defects.

The empirical study of Latin American television was aided by information and data made available by the Federal Communications Commission and the United States Information Agency. Unfortunately, the private media corporations were not so helpful.

This work was greatly facilitated by a National Defense Education Act Title IV fellowship at Washington University. Colleagues at Tulane University have greatly encouraged its completion and my immediate environment at Newcomb College has provided working conditions that have made the task more tolerable. Some of the material presented in this work has previously appeared in article form. It is reprinted here by permission of Routledge and Kegan Paul, Ltd. (for the *British Journal of Sociology*) and the *Indian Journal of Sociology*.

Finally, I wish to thank my wife, Lois, for her support—including hours of typing early drafts, proofreading, and similar unrewarding chores. Even more, she and my children must be thanked for providing the distractions from unrelenting work that are so vital to sanity.

contents

PART II.
THE NEW MEDIA AND DEVELOPMENT:
A CASE STUDY OF TELEVISION IN LATIN AMERICA

list of tables

list of diagrams

1.

introduction

COMMON OBSERVATIONS ON THE EMPIRICAL WORLD

In the twentieth century most of us are ready to concede that we live in a shrinking world and a secular planet stripped of its powers of enchantment. The idea of the diminishing world is in part the bias of the rich nations, and by it we mean that the distance between one international airport and the next, when measured in hours, is constantly being reduced. By means of telegraph, radio, and television, events anywhere in the world, diplomacy permitting, can be brought instantaneously into the homes of the electronically equipped. In this sense the world is indeed "small."

But this smallness doesn't necessarily mean we live in an increasingly unitary world. The very "closeness" of nations to each other makes global tensions more acute, or at least more keenly felt in our day-to-day consciousness. The cold war, with its fierce

1

ideological offshoots, is perhaps subjectively a more real form of conflict than, for example, the aristocratic sporting wars of the past that involved few non-combatants and were of short duration. The United Nations Organization, unfortunately, cannot provide a united world ideology under these conditions, despite its forays into human rights and welfare concerns. Instead it becomes a forum, or media studio, for world conflicts. But although ideologies of the different member nations conflict, they have a common basis. Since Tibet was reabsorbed as a Chinese province, no otherworldly theocratic states exist; modern states are invariably materialistic. That is, they all seek material development even though the distribution of the yield and the method to be employed are strong points of contention.

It is this materialism, coupled with worldwide communication, that accounts for much of the surface "sameness" that confronts the affluent world traveler. The search for the strange and exotic becomes more and more difficult. The traveler finds that it is difficult indeed to avoid the familiar. Nor is this just because tourism is now virtually a global industry that aims to make the tourist "at home" while taking him far from it. Rather, it seems, the tastes of the once colorful locals are now themselves only shades of cosmopolitan grey. Their material culture is only less plentiful and sometimes of poorer quality. When they are made locally, the blue jeans may fade sooner, and the carbonated drinks may go flat quicker than the "Western" product. Thus the imitated "modern" product may disappoint the sophisticated consumer. It is nonetheless a phenomenon that may have great implications for the material development of poorer countries.

The Western observer, of course, notices other differences between his home and the poor country that he visits. If the locals are not dismissed as "lazy," it may be noticed that fewer seem to be employed productively, and those that are seem less skilled than their counterparts (if any) at home, and they often employ less sophisticated technologies. Their poverty therefore is commonly attributed to low productivity. While this is not the whole explanation, it is accepted here as basically and self-evidently true.

Theoretical work on development habitually calls forth rather loose and abstract talk of modernization, industrialization, and economic development, while ignoring the commonly observed phenomena outlined above. This flaw, it is claimed, mars not only the work of systems and evolutionary theorists, but of those employing historical, typological (including "stage" theorists), and psychological approaches as well. As consumerism and producerism,[1] these two basic phenomena will be conceptualized as more than "common-sense" observations, and will then be used in constructing an alternate theory of development.

SOCIAL SCIENTIFIC APPROACHES
TO THE CHANGING WORLD

Social scientists have been interested in the general process of historical change and the birth of new institutions and personality types at various times in the past. Since World War II such interests have been greatly stimulated by the liberation of colonies, the formation of the United Nations, expanded world trade, and Western involvement in development projects.

The demands of governments, international organizations, and corporations for the services of social scientists prompted the theoretically inclined macro sociologist to apply to the underdeveloped countries the methods and concepts that had been used to analyze Western societies. He had a number of options. First, there was the historical approach, either unicausal, perhaps relying on the idea of metaphysical *Zeitgeist,*[2] or more particularistic, stressing the uniqueness of historical events. The dichotomic approach or a variation of it that employs the idea of a continuum between polar types of society—for example, folk-urban, sacred-secular, traditional-modern, and so on—has also been popular. It has deep roots in the sociological tradition of European sociology and was used by many "classical" thinkers including Auguste Comte,[3] Emile Durkheim,[4] and Ferdinand Tonnies.[5] Robert Redfield's study[6] of four Mexican settlements, a city, town, village, and tribe, and his conceptualization of a folk-urban continuum helped establish the European tradition in American thought. Parsons' pattern variables[7] are a multidimensional development from this method, as are the more refined "stages" approaches.[8]

The problems of using the dichotomic method stem from viewing the polar types as real rather than ideal type societies. The heuristic model is static, while all real societies are constantly undergoing change, albeit at different rates. Wilbert Moore, for example, has noted that current theories of modernization often employ a three-stage model: a static premodern, transitional, and what he calls a "nonsensically static" modernized stage.[9] The emphasis is on the changes in the society during the transitional stage, but the polar reference points, claims Moore, are too artificial to be very useful. This unilinear approach has reawakened interest in once discredited evolutionary theories. Indeed a conference and volume explicitly using such a model for development have been produced.[10] The problem, however, lies in empirically determining end points of the continuum. Traditional or premodern societies are not all alike,[11] nor can the "modern" destination of transitional societies be clearly predicted. Thus to apply evolutionary schema satisfactorily, there is apparently a need for many continua, which greatly distracts from the original parsimony of the dichotomic approach.

The general systems school has found in development studies a large subject for its grand theory and has shifted the focus of inquiry from structures to norms and values, while a few psychologists have approached the subject purely from the standpoint of the individual in society. Because sociologists and anthropologists have often been brought into development studies to aid economists, economic concepts have often served as models for new conceptualization. Thus, we are confronted with the concepts of political or social development and modernization at the macro level, and political, industrial, or achieving man as tools for the individualistic approach.

The many approaches to the development field have produced uneven results. While the literature in the area is often fascinating—perhaps because of its "exotic" subject matter—and is often well written, its findings are at best "illuminating." The virtuosity of scholars itself has hindered the collection of cumulative knowledge. More importantly, vague and idiosyncratic conceptualization, together with artificial distinctions between "macro" and "micro" levels of analysis, has added to the fragmentation of findings and hindered their application.

AN OUTLINE OF THE STUDY

In this section the purpose of the analysis, the theoretical orientation involved, the reasons for selecting the case study, and the organization plan of what follows are briefly outlined.

Purpose of the Work. The aim of this study is to establish a theory of development using the two concepts, "consumerism" and "producerism," that are refinements of commonly observed empirical phenomena. Its utility will be demonstrated by using it to clarify and critique the plethora of existing development theory, and to help bridge the hiatus between current macro and micro formulations. After its implications for the more specialized communications theories of development have been considered, its utility for examining the developmental uses of the mass media is demonstrated. This involves an empirical and comparative case study of television in seventeen Latin American countries. In this study the concepts of consumerism and producerism are used as heuristic devices.

Theoretical Orientation. Because there are no concepts and theories of development generally agreed upon by leading developmentalists, there is little orthodoxy in the field. The student faces a confusing array of possible orientations. My own approach is one of synthesis; of relating or joining different analytic levels, more and less abstract ideas. From the more abstract "macro" formulations, I focus attention on the phenomena of "consumerism" and "producerism." These are related to the less abstract and more psychological (or "micro") formulations of E. E. Hagen, D. C. McClelland, J. A. Kahl, and A. Inkeles.

The contemporary setting of development is stressed throughout. What is apparent to less scholarly observers is often overlooked by evolutionists and stage theorists alike. I refer to the often overlooked fact that "new" and "undeveloped" countries today do not become modern in the same way as the already industrialized nations did. There is a phasing of the new and disparate elements of "modernity" that is radically different from that experienced in the past by the now "advanced" countries. Television[12] now comes to the poor countries before factories or trans-country highways, and washing machines arrive in the modern sector before the widespread amenity of uncontaminated piped water. Those who ignore these disparities tend to think of the "nation" as a unitary system. A more empirical view of most nations would recognize several more or less modernized sectors in each country. Contemporary nations no longer exist in isolation. Rather than viewing the underdeveloped country as an integrated national system, we might more accurately—albeit with considerable simplification—recognize the Third World cities as the metropolitan satellites of the developed world, each with its underdeveloped "national" empire in the rural hinterlands. Clearly though, the general population is not left in its isolated traditionalism; even the backward sectors are partially modern or "transitional" as Lerner has put it.[13]

External international effects have inadvertently influenced the development of nations. There are probably no cases of wholly indigenous development, and models proposing it are avoided here. In the "developing" countries the methods of production and styles of consumption are shaped, if not wholly determined, by external practices. Indeed, the autonomous development of even the "first" industrial nation, England, has been persuasively questioned by Hobsbawm.[14] The developing countries of today must similarly contend with pressures from other governments and foreign enterprises. In addition, they are faced with two new phenomena influencing their development: financial aid from international agencies and foreign governments, and the intrusion of alien (sometimes international) corporations whose range of interests are extremely diffuse.

These external influences are sometimes imposed, but more often in part solicited. They are diffused to modern and transitional segments of society, both by direct observation of local pacesetters and by the impact of the mass communications media. Consumer styles are apparently transferred easily, but new productive skills diffuse more slowly. In addition, the former are more strongly encouraged from outside. This differential diffusion is not totally irrational for the internal consumer in the modern sector nor for the foreign enterprises. For many individuals and enterprises can thrive even in the absence of society-wide economic development.

Communication theories of development similarly provide a limited orientation. Contemporary theories including the work of Daniel Lerner, Wilbur Schramm, Karl W. Deutsch, Ithiel de Sola Pool, and H. Marshall McLuhan are examined. It is claimed that attention to the consumerism and producerism effects of the modern media helps prevent the all too common assumption that the presence of such media automatically aids economic development.

The Selection of the Case Study. The Latin American region was chosen because it has a wide range of national economies in terms of economic levels (as indicated by Gross National Product per capita) and growth rates. The richest countries—Venezuela, Argentina, and Uruguay—are relatively affluent, while the poorest—Haiti—is poor even by global standards. The fastest growing economies, for example, Mexico, have managed sustained development for more than a decade, even though the problem of stagnation faces most of the nations. The region also has political diversity within the "Western" pattern, but provides some controls through its cultural uniformities. The countries have similar, if not identical, histories, languages, religious institutions, and relationships to the rest of the world. In addition, data on Latin America are more plentiful and probably more reliable than for other underdeveloped regions.

The region is also the unofficial sphere of cultural, economic, and political influence for the world's richest nation, the United States. Thus, in terms of external influences this is an extreme case—the disparities between normal consumerism in the host country and that of the foreign influence source is maximized.

Television was chosen as the primary communications channel to be investigated because it is the most "modern" and technologically advanced medium, and has the most powerful potential effect on its audience, even if it is not at the moment the most commonly used. Seventeen countries (excluding Cuba) in the region have television broadcasting with varying levels of receiver density (sets per 1000 people). The United States has considerable interests in Latin American television, although this varies considerably by country, while other developed countries having media interests overseas (Britain, France, Japan) are not very active in this area. Thus it is the most "commercial" brand of television institution that is transferred into the region.

The Organization of the Study. Part I attempts to lay the foundation for a sociological theory of economic development. Chapter 2 is a review of current theory, most of which is found unsatisfactory. An alternative scheme is suggested in Chapter 3. The remaining chapter in Part I outlines the relevance of consumerism and producerism to communications theories of development. A modified communications theory is developed for heuristic use in the case study.

Part II is the empirical section of the study. It employs qualitative data primarily from U.S. trade magazines, and quantitative data from government, international, and private sources.

In this section the institutional characteristics of communications media and their development impact are examined. The media in Latin America, particularly the effect of United States government and corporations on Latin American television, are given detailed attention. North American influence is not, of course, the only force in the underdeveloped countries. Japanese, British, French, German, and other enterprises are also minimally involved. The United States was chosen because it is the leader in fashioning Western developmental rhetoric. Due to its military and economic power its actions are probably of more import, and Latin America is its unofficial sphere of influence for historical and geographical reasons (Britain and France apparently concentrate most of their activities in Africa, while Japan is active primarily in other Asian countries). I shall look for both consumerism and producerism potentials of the media. To assume that either consumerism or producerism is synonymous with modernization and lead, in time, to development is to overlook the problematic and potentially dys-economic nature of excess consumerism. The effects of the latter type will therefore receive most attention.

Chapter 5 is devoted to the quantitative aspects of the region's media and their relation to the economy. Latin America has wide inter- (as well as intra-) country variations in each case. The next chapter outlines United States interests in the region's television broadcasting industry. In Chapter 7 the chief characteristics of United States domestic television operation are sketched so that the degree and meaning of institutional transfer—via United States holdings in Latin America and imitation of United States practices by domestic companies in the region—can be gauged. In Chapter 8, the linkages between the television industry, advertising agencies, and United States corporate investment are investigated, and their implications for development are explored. This will be followed by a final chapter in which I shall summarize the developmental use of the media (including educational television) and its potential in the region.

NOTES

1. These two concepts are defined and developed in Chapter 3.
2. The "spirit" of the times, for example, the ages of reason, progress, secularization,

ideology, etc. Although there are often trends in societies that may be legitimately summarized by reference to the *Zeitgeist*, it should not be reified. If it is, what was first a useful descriptive device becomes an explanatory variable, and attention is distracted from the structural causes of change.

3. Theological-military society to the scientific-industrial, with a transitory metaphysical stage. See R. Aron, *Main Currents in Sociological Thought,* vol. I (New York: Basic Books, 1965), chap. II.
4. Societies characterized by mechanical and organic solidarity. Emile Durkheim, *The Division of Labor in Society,* trans. by G. Simpson (New York: Free Press Paperback Edition, 1964), pp. 70-132.
5. The polar types were called *Gemeinschaft* and *Gesellschaft*. His major work has been translated and edited by Charles P. Loomis. Ferdinand Tonnies, *Community and Society* (New York: Harper Torchbook, 1963).
6. Robert Redfield, *The Folk Culture of Yucatan* (Chicago: University of Chicago Press, 1941).
7. Talcott Parsons, *The Social System* (Glencoe, Ill.: Free Press, 1951). Also see his "Pattern Variables Revisited," *American Sociological Review,* 25 (1960), pp. 467-483.
8. The most important example is W. W. Rostow's *The Stages of Economic Growth* (New York: Cambridge University Press, 1960).
9. Wilbert E. Moore, "Developmental Change in Urban Industrial Societies," in Art Gallaher, Jr. (ed.), *Perspectives in Developmental Change* (Lexington: University of Kentucky Press, 1968), pp. 201-230.
10. H. R. Barringer, G. I. Blanksten, and R. W. Mack (eds.), *Social Change in Developing Areas* (Boston: Schenkman, 1965). An elegant rebuttal of the usefulness of organic and evolutionary models in studies of social change is the thesis of R. A. Nisbet, *Social Change and History* (New York: Oxford University Press, 1969).
11. As the work of ethnographers well illustrates, there is great variability between "premodern" cultures. This extends to their economic organization. See, for example, Manning Nash, *Primitive and Peasant Economic Systems* (San Francisco: Chandler, 1966).
12. This is even more the case with radio. For its spread in isolated regions of Peru, see William F. Whyte and Lawrence K. Williams, *Toward an Integrated Theory of Development* (Ithaca: New York State School of Industrial and Labor Relations, Cornell University, ILR Paperback, No. 5, February, 1968), p. 60.
13. Daniel Lerner, *The Passing of Traditional Society* (New York: Free Press, 1958).
14. E. J. Hobsbawm, *Industry and Empire* (New York: Pantheon, 1968).

Part I

A Sociological Theory of Economic Development

2.

critique
of developmental
concepts and theories

Industrialization has been a common starting point and focus for students of development. A technological determinism has been frequently maintained by those who argue for convergence of social forms with increasing industrialization. The introduction of mechanized production methods into traditional societies will elicit, it is held, "new societal patterns... [which] ... will resemble, in time, certain dominant patterns of western industrial society, which *may not be rejected by any people who accept the machines of the West*"[1] (author's italics). Industrialization, then, may be said to have a Westernizing effect. Some of these Western patterns are said to be the formation of purely economic roles and a new societal hierarchy, more personal material goods, machine-determined organization of work, and the shift to "modern" orientations in terms of the Parsonian variables. Similarly, Kerr *et al.*[2] have identified a "logic of industrialization" that demands a "wide range of skills and professional competency" and the predominance of achievement valuation in the allotment of occupation. This, it is claimed, replaces ascription on the basis of race, caste, family, and sex, and leads to the development of an open society.

This neo-Marxist (albeit Americanized) position of technological determinism has been seriously questioned. Blumer, for example, finds that the evidence "points clearly to the conclusion that industrialization, by its very make-up, can have no definite social effect."[3] He therefore proposes a counter theory, perhaps exaggerated, of the *Neutrality of Industrialization*: Composition of the work force and recruitment are to a large degree shaped by preexisting patterns of social interaction.[4] Similarly, the nature of the industrial milieu and conditions of life outside of the work place are claimed to be determined by society rather than by industry. Of course, Blumer admits, large-scale industry can determine the agglomeration of workers in larger settlements than had their rural life. But subsequent changes in life style and the acceptance of new ideologies should, claims Blumer, be attributed to "urbanization" rather than "industrialization."

Another of the doubters of "harnassed" change theories, Clifford Geertz, claims the autonomy of "economic modernization" from "cultural patterns and social structures."[5] Singer questions the inseparability of Western values and technology. He considers that the "battle between 'traditionalism' and 'industrialism' is a clash of hypothetical constructs which do not realistically reflect the obstacles to economic development."[6] These constructs, it may be added, may be inapplicable because they were formulated primarily to account for the rise of early capitalism, and not for the diffusion of Western values and technology to the non-Western world.[7] Nash also doubts the contingency, not of industrialization, but of economic development itself, with changes in social structure,[8] and is particularly dubious of the pattern variable approach.

The concept of "social development" is attacked by Blumer.[9] It is used, perhaps, to legitimize the field of study for sociologists and to give them equal standing with economic developmentalists. In practice, however, it is "made synonymous with modernization." The latter, claims Blumer, is a historically and spacially limited concept, but is quite legitimate if the characteristics of modernism can be isolated and "the mechanisms that bring group life into conformity with . . ." these can be traced. Thus, if "modernization" is rigorously specified, it has some validity, but "social development" has none.

It has been shown that attempts to trace various changes in society from technological changes has drawn strong criticism from others in the development field. Too much is *assumed* to accompany, or be defined into, industrialization. Too many concepts are vague, and as Blumer has shown for "social development," are often overlapping or synonymous with others. This conceptual confusion is illustrated by the following examination of macro or societal concepts as they are presented by their leading exponents.

THE WORK OF THE MACRO THEORISTS

S. N. Eisenstadt. Modernization is the key concept used by Eisenstadt. It is all embracing and subsumes both economic development and industrialization. Third World countries, he says, have seldom opposed modernization, whose processes include the expansion of education, economic development, industrialization, and rural development.[10] But he omits consideration of the crucial differential rates of expansion of these processes, sectoral imbalance, and the priority of individualistic interests over public welfare. True, very few people can be found who categorically oppose the "good (material) life" in general, but this vaguely held value complex is not sufficient to place societal goals in the fore.

Nazi Germany and the Perón regime are cited by Eisenstadt as breakdowns in modernization (perhaps he means "democratization," "westernization," or a similar, more limited term). But surely Hitler's regime had some tangible achievements in the economic modernization of the country. While heavy military expenditure inflates the GNP, thereby rendering it a spurious indicator of material well-being, the war product was put to use to facilitate what might be termed "development by conquest." Nazi expenditures on public works, including those spent to build Europe's most advanced highway network, can scarcely be classified as breakdowns in modernization. Perón, even if not "modern" by Eisenstadt's estimation, did indeed attempt to change sectoral imbalances and this, presumably, is a "modern" enough endeavor. Neither is it clear that he categorically opposed mass education, industrialization, and economic development. Indeed he was very much "for" these things. Certainly the Perón years were not a return to "tradition," but a period of change in the balance between Eisenstadt's components of modernization. The two regimes could be viewed as "breakdowns" in modernization if Eisenstadt had proposed a sequence involving his elements of modernization, but his *gestalt* view of the latter makes this impossible.

In a more recent work, Eisenstadt maintains a Western conception of modernization that posits simultaneous social, political, and economic development. He recognizes, however, the disharmonies in underdeveloped countries, which he attributes to "structural duality"—the uneven development between "disorganized traditional" and "unintegrated" modern sectors.[11] Thus developing countries are undergoing pathological growth patterns, while the West, he apparently assumes, developed "normally" in a balanced and integrated manner.

Reinhard Bendix. Bendix gives nominal definitions for both industrialization and modernization, which are his two key concepts. The first refers to the "technical-economic," the latter to the "socio-political" changes familiar to us from the recent history of Western Europe. Thus he is consciously using a Western model of developmental change. Industrialization is defined as those "economic changes brought about by a technology based on inanimate sources of power [mechanization?] as well as on the continuous development of applied scientific research." Modernization, which he admits often goes under the name of social and political development,

> ... refers to all those social and political changes that accompanied industrialization in many countries of Western civilization. Among these are urbanization, changes in occupational structure, social mobility, development of education—as well as political changes from absolutist institutions to responsive and representative governments [democratization?] and from a laissez-faire to a modern welfare state.[12]

He cannot, of course, say how much of each change accompanies a given degree of industrialization. He is concerned rather with gross historical trends. Note, however, that the modernization elements he cites are the "good things" that (after an unspecified time lag) accompanied industrialization. He doesn't, for example, consider the development of totalitarian police methods, mass armies equipped with the latest sophisticated weaponry, or imperialism as modernization, yet they too accompanied industrialization in the West.

The Western *gestalt,* however, is not being repeated *en masse* in the Third World as Bendix himself well demonstrates. (In fairness to him it should be noted that his concepts are not used as descriptions of reality or analytical constructs but as "benchmarks" from which to examine the empirical world.) The political components of modernization even in the West European, Russian, and Japanese cases are, he admits, "too differentiated to be compatible with neo-evolutionist assumptions."[13] So modernization as defined by him is not, in fact, a single coherent process: Urbanization, democratization, and the shift to welfarism do not develop simultaneously. Neither do the "industrial" and "modern" processes mesh well together. Modernization doesn't necessarily "accompany industrialization" today. It may possibly lag behind (China and the more repressive Middle-eastern states) or as is more often the case, precede industrialization (at least in the "modern" sectors of poor countries).

Wilbert E. Moore. Moore's mature position is perhaps best outlined in his small but in many ways remarkable book entitled *The Impact of Industry.* He attempts to find a middle ground between what he calls the "convergence" and "divergence" schools of thought; those who argue that common technology will lead to common cultures (for example, Inkeles, Bauer, Rose, Kerr, and Moore himself at an earlier date); and those who say that it won't (for example, Blumer and Bendix). He also criticizes the dichotomic approach, arguing that neither "traditional" nor "modern" societies are static, a view fostered by what he calls "the functional equilibrium error."[14] The intellectual honesty of this statement can be admired only when we remember that Moore spent the greater part of his long career as a leading exponent of functionalism. Unfortunately though, he does little to improve our conceptual tools.

He defines industry as "fabrication of raw materials into intermediate components or finished products by primarily mechanical means dependent on inanimate sources of power."[15] Industrialization is apparently the increase in industry. Moore broadens this concept to include the *consumption* of products. This definition, if we exclude the addition, has the makings of a concrete concept, but this is apparently not Moore's concern. He argues, for example, that "several terms are often *and properly* [my italics] used interchangeably, though their meaning differs [sic] in detail."[16] It is this brand of fuzziness—the interchangeability of concepts—that so plagues the study of development.

Like Eisenstadt, Moore's most comprehensive term is "modernization."[17] Its reference may be political, social, or economic and it means joining the "common pool of world knowledge and useful techniques." It involves using the "latest organizational procedures" in crime control, mass communication, public health, education, transport, and so forth; in sum, joining the "modern world." Clearly though, too much is involved here to permit the use of his definition of modernization as an analytical concept. It is unclear which phenomena essentially constitute the "modern world" (even of knowledge) that the unintegrated must join, and clearly many separate processes are involved. The emphasis on the "latest" procedures is also confusing. For example, are we to assume the latest police methods in the United States, France, or Russia are the most modern?

Marion Levy. Levy employs the term "modernization" in a more precise way than the writers so far considered. It should be noted, however, that his usage resembles what Moore and Bendix would call "industrialization." His definition "hinges on the uses of inanimate sources of power and the use of tools to multiply the effect of effort."[18] He visualizes two continua—inanimate power and tool use—on which all societies can be placed. Modernization is presumably the process of increasing usage of power and (or?) tools. There are concomitants of modernization, we are told. For example, if stability is to be maintained, centralization must accompany it. Modernization in the West, for example, went hand in hand with an emphasis on science, increased specialization and interdependence, materialistic ethics, objective recruitment, and bureaucratization;[19] and these, at least by implication, are assumed to accompany modernization elesewhere. Economic development is presumably an outcome of modernization.

David Apter. In his book dedicated to Marion Levy, Apter gives a more abstract view of the major concepts. Like Bendix, he starts by investigating the Western origins of modernity. Modernization, he says, "first occurred . . . through the twin processes of commercialization and industrialization" and led to a wide range of social changes. These changes may be seen as the triumph of reason, which when "applied to human affairs is the foundation of modernity."[20] But Apter realizes that modernization has not been induced by the same "forces" universally:

> In many non-Western areas modernization has been the result of commercialization and, rather than industrialization, bureaucracy. Modernization can thus be seen as something apart from industrialization—caused by it in the West but causing it in other areas.[21]

He thus raises the argument for concrete and independent conceptualization of these terms. Unfortunately, however, he contributes little toward this end.

First, Apter's definitions are extremely obscure. Modernization is "the process of consciously directing and controlling the social consequences of increased role differentiation and organized complexity in a society."[22] But what are these "consequences"? And what is it that induces "complexity" at the outset? Perhaps the latter is industrialization, for although Apter defines this as an "aspect of modernization,"[23] it nevertheless modifies dysfunctional institutions and customs by creating new machine-based roles and "social instruments." Industrialization is claimed to be "more dynamic" than modernization, but "more narrowly consistent in its processes." It is by no means clear how industrialization can be "more dynamic" than modernization and yet be an "aspect" of it.

The three major concepts—a development, modernization, and industrialization—are conceived on three different levels of abstraction, but relate somewhat ambiguously to the same social phenomena. The confusion here can be demonstrated by quoting Apter at length:

> Development, modernization, and industrialization, although related phenomena, can be placed in descending order of generality. Development, the most general, *results from* the proliferation and integration of functional roles in a community. Modernization *implies* three conditions—a social system that can constantly innovate without falling apart (and that includes among its essential

beliefs, the acceptability of change); differentiated, flexible social structures; and a social framework to provide the skills and knowledge necessary for living in a technologically advanced world. Industrialization, a special aspect of modernization, may be defined as the *period* in a society in which the strategic functional roles are related to manufacturing. It is possible to attempt the modernization of a given country without much industry, but it is not possible to industrialize without modernization.[24] [All italics are mine.]

We are not told here what development and modernization *are,* only what the former *results from,* and the latter *implies.* These are hypothetical relationships of abstract concepts rather than mutually independent classifications of empirical phenomena. Industrialization is defined as a *period* during which certain changes take place rather than the change processes themselves. The static nature of the entire statement—its stress on integration and lack of attention to the processes of change and disharmony—clearly demonstrates what Moore courageously called the "functional equilibrium error."

The different ways in which the major developmental terms are used and related to each other by the writers so far discussed is summarized in Diagram 1 (diagrams located at end of book). The referent for each concept is that of its author. Thus, for example, "Modernization" obviously does not mean the same thing throughout the diagram. It illustrates that what little consensus exists in the field extends only to the nomenclature, not to the content of the key concepts.

Horowitz, Germani, and others have recognized the need for clearer conceptualization of developmental concepts and the possible disparities between them. Their work will now be examined.

I. L. Horowitz. Horowitz has written of the difficulty of "equating the development process with the presence of . . . modernization." Why one should wish to *equate* the two is not clear—unless there is a wish to make one of the two obsolete. The relationship between the two is, however, a valid field of inquiry and does require clearer conceptualization, as Horowitz points out. But both terms, not just the one Horowitz examines, should be clarified. He delineated the imprecision of the term "modernization" in the following manner:

A standard definition . . . usually includes at least the following: a belief in the primacy of science, or at least *in the products of applied engineering* [my italics]; a belief in a secular way of conducting affairs; and belief in the need for continuing changes in society and economy.[25]

He adds that modernization may also mean the creation of a national culture. Thus, he concludes it ". . . may be science for some and imperialism for others." The confusion here is probably due to the failure of development scholars to conceptualize nation-building (or "empire-building")[26] separately. Nation-building is not necessarily "modern"; indeed it can be argued that dissolution of artificial polities (for example, Nigeria and the Indian subcontinent) into several more homogeneous nation states is the more rational, and hence modern, course to take. The belief in "progress" and the products of applied engineering—namely, Western consumer goods and welfare benefits—does not necessarily lead to a belief in science. *Belief in* anything is also a static conception, while we clearly need a processual concept.

The need for a clear separation of the three major developmental concepts is manifested both by the failure of earlier formulations to serve as analytical tools, and by a recognition that *sectors* of Third World economies are indeed "modern," while their economies as a whole are neither industrial nor developing.

In his *Three Worlds of Development*, Horowitz pointed clearly to this sectoral nature of modernization and criticized the overlapping and confused formulations of earlier theorists. But as has been shown, the concepts were not explicitly redefined in this work. His most explicit statement on the distinction between the concepts is found elsewhere. Indicators for modernization and industrialization are posited, and the possible incongruence of the two demonstrated by reference to Argentina. Thus he concludes,

> development might be said to encompass a double interchange—the interaction of modernization and industrialization forming the core problems of developmental processes and strategies alike.[27]

He then stresses imperialism (fostered by military coups) as a prime cause of modernization. The formulation of clear definitions of the three concepts and their interrelationships are not, however, within the scope of his article.

Gino Germani. Germani has also recognized that modernization (or rather aspects of it) can retard industrialization and be detrimental to economic development. But he too is not very precise or consistent in his use of these concepts. Until recent years in Latin America, he says,

> ... modernization affected only small groups of elites in the central areas of each country. The process of development today affects the entire population and invades the whole national territory. Furthermore, the process has acquired unprecedented velocity.[28]

"Development" here is equated with "modernization." The "demonstration effect," he continues, is pervasive throughout society and leads to

> ... a consumption orientation [modernization?] which is imitative of highly developed countries, under conditions in which the productive machinery [industrialization?] is still in a state of underdevelopment ... [and] ... in a period in which the "take off" [to sustained economic development?] has not yet occurred.[29]

In a later empirical work, however, Germani has lost sight even of this basic consumption/production imbalance.[30] There is little evidence in his article on Argentine immigration that he clearly separates the major developmental terms. Instead, modernization is again used as an all-embracing and vague concept. Immigration is the focus of the study, and Germani makes a good case for its uniqueness in Argentina. The influx there was much heavier relative to the native population than in any other country. It was a "powerful factor" in the total process of modernization and led to a massive "realignment" of the population in social, political, and economic terms. This had been the aim of the early modernizers of Argentina who wanted to pattern the country after the advanced Western countries of the time, France and Britain. To do this they encouraged (1) mass immigration, with the idea that importing Westerners would make the country modern; (2) universal and compulsory education; and (3) the "modernization" of agriculture, importation of capital, and the development of what Walt W. Rostow would call an "infrastructure." The early attempt to modernize failed, Germani claims, because of insufficient immigration. For the boom period after 1853, he tries to determine the contribution of immigration alone (the other modernizing steps listed above are neglected in his analysis) to the nation's modernization.

He outlines three ways that immigration aided modernization in this period: First, it provided labor for industrial establishments, the construction of the infrastructure, and farm modernization, which led to economic growth and (he uses the term loosely) modernization. That their labor was important cannot be denied, but Germani ignores the impetus for making employment available. Later in the article it becomes clear that immigrants were disproportionately the founders of non-agricultural enterprises. Second, immigration induced value changes in the society at large. Germani is reluctant to deny that the immigrants were *not* "moderns," although he himself clearly outlines their origins. They were heavily peasant and unskilled workers primarily from Italy and Spain and both countries were "backward" compared to Northern Europe at the time. (Spain of course still is, and the neo-renaissance in Italy is a very recent phenomenon.) Rather than *being* modern, their urban enclosure—due to both archaic and "modern" commercial land tenure systems—and the fact that they had already broken from tradition by emigrating, *made them* so.

Finally, immigration is claimed to have led to the "modernization" of the stratification system. By this, Germani means the formation of a middle class. But this was probably due more to urbanization and commercial expansion (in which the immigrants admittedly took the largest part) than immigration *per se*. Germani's long and tenuous discussion of assimilation is possibly also misplaced. He is too concerned with Eisenstadt's absorption model in attempting to determine the impact of the immigrants on the native stratification system, when his own data point clearly to the fact that it is the urban sector—predominantly immigrant and first-generation—that is absorbing the older Argentines.

The overall connection of the concepts used by Germani is apparently as follows: The presence of modern individuals (immigrants) promotes industrialization, which leads to economic development and ultimately modernization. This is clearly not the relationship suggested more recently by Horowitz. Urbanization and marginality (in Everett E. Hagen's sense) are perhaps better explanations of Argentine development. The sectoral nature (and contemporary stagnation) of the economy must also be explained. The "immigrants," due to their urban residence and employment, are in the "modern" sector. But as Germani admits, this had been geared to domestic consumption. It has not been converted to a cosmopolitan modernity by the successful immigrant alone. The fashion-setting aristocracy and old Argentine *commercial* farmer have contributed heavily to the demand for sophisticated imported goods, to the detriment of local manufacturers and national equality. This "new modernism" is completely overlooked by Germani.

To use the distinction between modernization and industrialization hinted at in the work of Horowitz and Germani, it remains necessary to clarify the terms in order to build a theory of development. To do this it appears necessary to break down and limit existing concepts. More than historical analyses[31] of the terms are needed if they are to be more than generalized rubrics.[32] To redefine the concepts would perhaps only add to existing confusions, and to multiply terms by talking of "breakdowns in modernization," "demodernization," or "remodernization"[33] again does little for clarity. In Chapter 3, therefore, I shall extract elements from existing conceptions to form concepts that are reasonable entities. The consumer/producer elements noted by Horowitz and Germani are the basis for this reformulation.

INDIVIDUALISTIC AND PSYCHOLOGICAL APPROACHES

Despite the value and perhaps greater importance of structural factors in explaining development, the individual, his thought and action, should be part of the analysis. It is of course a truism, even if it is often overlooked, that *people,* not abstract societies or structures, enact change.[34] The individual thoughts and acts of a person are of course shaped by others—conceptualized as structures, institutions, or more abstractly (though partially) as society. We thus would expect to find a relationship between types of society and the individuals composing it. Both the sociological schools of symbolic interactionism and the diverse findings of socialization studies provide evidence justifying this view. Similarly, the psychoanalytical-anthropological discipline of "culture and personality" supports it.

All individuals are not, however, equally exposed to the multiple elements of their society—so they are by no means all the same. In varying degrees they all help shape their society; at times some can radically alter it. Take, for example, the impact of the typically low-status assassin who kills a prominent figure in society. Any institutional positions held by the slain victim are of course refilled, but the personal qualities that the former holder added to the role are no longer present, and the whole character of the institution under new leadership may change.

Similarly a military coup may revolutionize the distribution of power in a society. There may be important structural prerequisites for such action, but it is nevertheless a mere handful of officers that decides who will compose the junta; and when, where, and how the coup will take place.

The attempts to account for economic development made by the "macro" theorists discussed so far have generally failed to take individual roles and role performances into consideration. Their work focused on and limited itself to a societal level of analysis. As such, it is abstract to the degree in which it is removed from empirically observed individual behavior. The work of psychologists and those who focus on individuals suffers from precisely the opposite malady. That is, rather than interpreting the macro abstractions and fashioning a more subtle view of development that treats both individual and structural reality, their work too often only yields a separate and rival level of explanation. It ignores the importance and tenacity of social structures, and in so doing is forced to move directly from observed behavior to macro prediction with no intervening variables. This inadequacy, it is suggested, points clearly to the need for a synthesis of micro and macro levels of analysis, a synthesis that is crucial to the future development of theories, if they are to be more closely tuned to empirical reality. After considering the shortcomings of micro approaches, my alternate formulation in Chapter 3 will attempt to move toward such a synthesis.

The need for "innovators" (in the sense of "those who do new things") to effect social changes can hardly be denied. But the investigator of them faces several dilemmas and many pitfalls. One of the latter is to assume that a certain group of men are indeed innovators (usually small businessmen), simplistically assume their function in society (that they induce economic growth), and then trace their origins and devise ways of generating more of them. These assumptions overlook the structural limitations on innovation. For example, it is difficult for a prison inmate, army recruit, or even a low-echelon bureaucrat to "innovate," no matter how innately innovative he may be.

The dilemmas confronting the micro theorist include the choice between mass and elite focus; shall economic or political change be attributed to the many (Marx, Weber) or the few (managerialism, political elite theorists)? In addition, should the innovator be considered normal ("modern man") or a deviant from the routine-oriented ("traditional") population? Are only those who effect "good" changes to be termed innovators, or can manifestly "dysfunctional" changes also be attributed to them? For those taking the individualistic approach, is innovation the outcome of distinct values or the marginality of their subject? The options taken by leading theorists on these dilemmas will become apparent in the discussion of the writers that follows.

McClelland and the Need for Achievement School

McClelland's work is based on the discovery of a motivational syndrome or drive previously overlooked by Freudians which he calls the "need for achievement" (nAch). The discovery was the result of laboratory testing, and further evidence was collected in his major work, *The Achieving Society.* [35] It is apparently a motive to achieve (irrespective of specific goals), but it is not the only cause of actual achievement since, we are told, "social approval, power, knowledge and ability factors" are also important. In the basic experiment two groups of students were given intelligence tests. One group had been told that the tests were based on official tests to measure intelligence and leadership, which is claimed to have aroused their achievement motive. The other group took the tests "cold." Differences between the groups were attributed to the achievement motive. Each group was then directed to write stories which were stimulated by showing them a series of pictures. Differences in the frequency of "standards of excellence" in them were attributed to the same increase in frequency over their "cold" fellows. The frequency count of achievement-related ideas in stories written under normal conditions has been taken as a measure of need for achievement.

Scores vary from one individual to the next, but in general it was found that the middle class in the United States scored higher than the "upper" and "lower" classes. The high scorers are not the routine types, but a combination of "go-getters" (work well for prizes) and team workers (perform well when cooperation must be obtained). In sum, they are entrepreneurial types. They are nourished, McClelland claims, by certain beliefs and childbearing practices in the family. He supplements his contemporary data with scores calculated from the fairy tales of ancient Greece, pre-Incan Peru, and England (1400-1800). Changes in the total nAch in these societies (it is perhaps doubtful that his scores are really this representative) were found to be positively related to subsequent economic development.

The only mediating factor given between the psychological measure and economic development is the presence of a large number of entrepreneurs. If we could only get more of them, says the author, "things would start to hum." McClelland has since conducted experiments in Kakinanda, India,[36] to increase the nAch of businessmen (who are, incidentally, already elite entrepreneurs). He is nonetheless interested in the common good, which he interprets as building up an entrepreneurial class, rather than strengthening dominant elites. He suggests that by improving education and public welfare (and perhaps updating nursery tales?) rapid economic development will commence in about twenty years. But can a wretchedly poor country like India invest its miserable resources in this way, and then wait so long for a return on its investment?

The problem with McClelland's causal chain is that high nAch leads to entrepreneurial (or if his laissez-faire bias is ignored, "innovative") activity only under very special conditions. There must be a possibility for achievement (pAch?), and the type of achievement both wanted and possible must be materially productive.[37] For example, it is conceivable that a middle-class entrepreneurial or modern segment of a society, although stimulating productivity, might also set up consumer strains in the economy and by demanding imported goods or their substitutes in fact *retard* development. Thus McClelland's formulation is of rather low utility both for explaining and for inducing economic development.

Psychological testing for "need for achievement" has been widely practiced. LeVine,[38] for example, summarizes studies carried out in

Japan, the United States, Brazil, Germany, and among the Eskimos and Ojibwa. His own work was in Nigeria—the testing from dream accounts of Ibo, Housa, and Yoruba schoolboys. Africans, he reports, are not traditional:

> ... we might accurately regard them as pragmatic frontiersmen with a persistent history of migration, settlement and resettlement of new lands and of responding to the challenges of intertribal wars and the slave trace.[39]

Presumably, then, they have entrepreneurial types, even though the national economy and growth rates are low. Thus Nigerian nAch scores were not found to be vastly different from those found in developed countries. Nor were tribal differences markedly apparent, even though the Ibo are collectively the most "commercial" group. Factors other than high nAch scores are therefore necessary to explain economic growth and levels.

Everett E. Hagen and Status Withdrawal

Like McClelland and his followers discussed above, Hagen also ends with the search for innovators. In his major work[40] he claims—with the exaggeration typical of those greatly troubled by the failings of their chosen profession—that economic theory is inadequate to the task of explaining growth. He turns instead to social and psychological factors. Social structure in his model shapes parental behavior. This determines the child-rearing patterns adopted by adults and "childhood environment" that molds the personalities of the young. It is personality, according to Hagen, that impels economic growth. The same order of criticism that was raised with respect to McClelland's work is applicable here. At the beginning of the causal chain, what causes "social structure" to change, and what are the linkages between "personality" and economic development? As with McClelland, innovators are offered as the latter link. But innovative personalities are not formed by "traditional" societies, claims Hagen.

He therefore looks at empirical cases of economic growth—in England, Japan, Colombia, Indonesia, Burma, and among the Sioux—to discover the sources of innovation. (It should be noted here that innovation is claimed to lead to "technological progress." Thus in his scheme the invention of improved technology is implicitly taken as the only method of economic development. Most poor countries today, of course, borrow their technology from the rich.) The idea that socially marginal persons are a source of innovation is widely believed. Hagen is more specific—he pinpoints those who have experienced status withdrawal, that is, downward mobility. This causes them to lose their traditional values but to still strive fanatically to regain their lost prestige. They still want the same ultimate ends, but use different means to achieve them. (McClelland is more reasonable and optimistic on this point—he believes that high aspirations can exist and be induced among the lowly.) To effect economic development one must presumably withdraw status (prestige) from segments of the population and then wait a few decades for them to "innovate"! Obviously the implications of this theory are none too practical. A revolutionary shake-up of rewards in a society may indeed stimulate growth, but not necessarily for the reasons Hagen would offer.

The Weber-Lipset Mass Value Approach

Max Weber[41] is usually regarded by sociologists as the father of the value approach to social change. His attempt was to explain the origin of a complex of beliefs and ideologies that he called the "Spirit of Capitalism." He suggests that it derived from the (Calvinist) "Protestant Ethic." Similarities in the two value sets were found (the common factors of industriousness, frugality, and the pre-eminence of a "calling"), but as Samuelson's[42] critique emphasizes, the hiatus between innerworldly religious asceticism and the totally secularized "spirit" could not be bridged. Indeed, Weber did not attempt to show the historical transformation of one to the other, but the affinity between them.

The transformation to the "spirit of capitalism" presumably should have been made by most Protestants, but apparently it was not (or structural factors prevented their rise to eminence). But large numbers of them were able to accumulate capital by fortuitous circumstances combined with asceticism and hard work—the crucial similarities of the "spirit" and "ethic." What made some successful entrepreneurs—that is, capable of taking risks—is unclear except that they wanted to "put their money to work." But clearly this can be done safely in conservative investments, for example, in land. The common argument for the Jews as economic entrepreneurs is more plausible for they were often forced to choose the more risky investments.

Lipset[43] has attempted to work within the Weberian framework, while supplementing it with other approaches including some consideration of structural factors. To this end he usefully brings together a mass of literature on the subject, but the "synthesis" is not entirely successful. Although he admits that both values and social structure are relevant to entrepreneurial and economic development, his emphasis is nonetheless on the former. On the positive side, he plausibly mediates the mass values as opposed to marginality/deviance dilemma. Building on Weber's findings for South Germany with data for Latin America and Canada, he concludes as follows: In cultures that favor and reward entrepreneurship, the innovators are drawn from the "mainstream" and they become culture heroes. Where the society is tradition-conscious (for example, French Canada and Latin America, which he characterizes as elitist, ascriptive, and particularistic), innovation is the mark of deviance and it is therefore marginals who adopt entrepreneurial roles (Jews and Protestants in French Canada, immigrants in Latin America).

His characterization of Latin America is admittedly highly general, but nonetheless overdrawn. True, there are aristocratic leanings in educational curricula and in career choices (relatively low enrollments in science and engineering), but the economies in the region are surely less "Iberian," traditional, and aristocratic than he portrays them. The upper class is no longer a traditional landed class, even though it may be descended from one. Commercial farming, city apartments, and investment in the international stock market—not land as Lipset claims—is the modern *forte* of this class. As Lipset admits, they want quick profits and low-risk investments—which is surely sound "modern" behavior, even if it works to the detriment of the country as a whole.

The main flaw in his argument is the imprecise use of the term "entrepreneur." Like other writers, he at times uses it to describe the type of nineteenth-century man who in McClelland's words could "really make things hum" (like the hero in H. G. Wells' novel of Victorian enterprise, *Tono Bungay,* the small capitalist who would stake everything on innovation). But today small businesses die fast. Perhaps we do not need this type at all in an age of calculated risks and governmental underwriting (or corporate purchase) of radical innovations. Indeed, the United States Agency for International Development (AID) will not finance risky—or what one official has termed "crackpot"—schemes overseas, so why should a rich cosmopolitan native? At other times, Lipset seems to be yearning for a universal distribution of American style businessmen and technicians. Technical skills are certainly needed in modern industrial societies, but in an age of bureaucratic science most technicians cannot be readily and unambiguously labeled "innovators," much less "entrepreneurs." Certainly the aristocratic values of a society may inhibit the selection of technology as a career, but the realistic assessment of rewards together with the limited number of university places and inferior facilities are structural limitations that are perhaps more important than individual values. Thus, seemingly anachronistic behavior may in fact have an entirely rational basis.

Finally, Lipset completely ignores the international setting of Latin America. Most countries, even in Latin America, *have had* a rapid development period. But foreign investment and expanded world trade may now inhibit domestic investment. Clearly it is wiser for an *individual* to invest in General Motors or Alfa Romeo stock, and to work in their Latin American affiliates than to try to build autos to compete with them.

Types of Entrepreneur: Cardoso

Cardoso's work is important here because it is a clear departure from the usually vague conceptions of what constitutes entrepreneurial activity, and the simplistic assumptions of its economic effects. His conception of entrepreneurial elites follows that of Weber—they are the groups of individuals who "direct modern economic organizations."[44] In Latin America, he notes, they are not revolutionary (the bourgeoisie-versus-aristocracy hypothesis of Marx); instead of being in open conflict with the traditional landed oligarchy, they have merged with it. In his interpretation, Latin America has entrepreneurial elites by definition. Cardoso is therefore concerned with their qualities, origins, and functions. He distinguishes between industrial, commercial, and agricultural elites and those having international or only domestic linkages.

In another article he concentrates on further differentiating types of industrial elites.[45] He classifies these according to their orientation toward their society at large (S+ or −) and toward their individual enterprises (E+ or −). The four possible types resulting from consideration of the two dichotomous attributes are as follows: (1) The *speculator* (S−, E−) who takes risks, manipulates stocks, and exploits labor; (2) the *puritan* entrepreneur (S−, E+) who is often of artisan origin but who will rationalize the operation of his own enterprise; (3) the *progressive* (S+, E−) who attempts to maximize his wealth by political influence of the market rather than rationalization of his enterprise; and (4) the *modern* (S+, E+) who pursues market manipulation and planning together with attempts to upgrade his company's efficiency. External conditions may favor one type over the others. Type 2, the puritan, clearly cannot compete with sophisticated large-scale enterprises, nor will his transformation to the "modern" type be feasible if foreign capital is invested early in the establishment of the industry. In the latter case, the domestic enterprise may require a type 4 organization from the start if it is to survive.

The distribution of these types is more a function of structural conditions than the qualities of individuals. Thus for Cardoso, the presence of many "speculators" does not imply poor moral fiber, but structural conditions unfavorable to industrial growth. The origin of the entrepreneurs is also attributed to the mode of integration of the economy into the world market, and internal social and political conditions. The concentration of sons of traders in these groups in Argentina is an example of the former (world market integration), while the similarly high proportion of sons of soldiers among entrepreneurs in that country is a reflection of the latter (political) conditions. Industrial entrepreneurs are therefore produced and their activity shaped by society.

The myth derived from early Western industrialization, namely, that the swelling of an entrepreneurial middle class leads to sustained economic growth, is seriously challenged by Cardoso's insistence on the importance of structural conditions. Bourricaud[46] has demonstrated the grip that a small elite (the Peruvian oligarchy) can have on the economy, while Ratinoff[47] notes that some countries are stagnant, yet have a middle class. In Latin America, he writes, the latter has in effect been co-opted and now calls more for the protection of private property than state intervention to curb the upper class. State welfare measures and education are urban-based and benefit the middle class. They therefore have vested interests in the status quo, and the parasitic modern sector of the economy. In sum, the middle class is too sophisticated to provide large numbers of risk-taking innovators, and as Andrew Frank has observed, the lower class is too poor save for "penny capitalism" in the tertiary sector.[48]

Traditional and Modern Man

In addition to the study of individual motivation and entrepreneurs, it has been popular to set up typologies of individual qualities—usually of the "traditional man"—"modern man" variety. Survey methods can then be used to gauge the frequency of each in any society. The limitations of this dichotomous view, but also the heuristic value of the approach, was demonstrated a decade ago by Lerner and his associates.[49] The work is based on the authors' field studies in Turkey, Lebanon, Egypt, Jordan, and Iran. It utilized a rich collection of interview data of individual attitudes and relates them to structural factors (with emphasis on the communications media). Lerner found that when he was actually confronted by villagers in the "field," the dichotomy was of little descriptive value. Rather, he found that he was faced with various types of "transitionals"—those, for example, who were receptive to the mass media but were illiterate.

The key to the breakdown of traditionalism (the title implies it is "passing," but the text indicates that it has already passed) is the media. We are given an extensive description of a "tradition" oriented village chief in Turkey. He expounds the military virtues of the bygone Turkish empire, hopes his sons will join the army and fight for their country in Korea, and scorns the commercialism of the village grocer. He has a radio, but doesn't think his family should be contaminated by listening to it, nor are they permitted to go to the movie theater. Four years later Lerner conducted a follow-up interview. Since the first encounter, the village had been linked to nearby Ankara by a bus service; the settlement had grown rapidly and was becoming a dormitory town for commuting city workers. The village chief was found to be much more receptive to change. He had even set up his two sons in village commerce selling modern (for example, canned food) goods! Apparently structural factors are more "powerful" than, and causally prior to, purely attitudinal ones.

The effect of the media is to bring the modern sector of the economy into the consciousness of all. This has a great impact on the individual. For example, Lerner tells of a seventeen-year-old Jordanian Bedouin who "saw an American movie once and has been restless ever since."[50] They see modernity, and rapidly come to want it:

> The Workers are Transitionals, showing the impact of modern drives. But they may be outrunning their social context. "Enjoy myself" and "Live a good life"—these are phrases appropriate to the consumer of abundance in a highly productive and widely participant society. On the lips of the workers in Egypt, where scarcity rules, these phrases may augur a time of troubles ahead. They bespeak desires that will not easily be satisfied.[51]

Lerner clearly recognizes here that "transitional" man gets modern tastes for consumption without becoming more productive, an observation that should be given more attention by those who continue to retain holistic views of modernity. Lerner and his associates found that in Egypt the gap between aspirations in general and realistic plans was "much greater than that of European nations in their formative stages [for the latter] ... did not have their aspirations set by the present Western model of military strength and economic prosperity."[52] Lerner is therefore also aware of the changing world context of development.

Inkeles[53] and Kahl[54] may be considered recent exponents of the dichotomic approach. The problem with using such conceptions of "total" attitude sets stems from their multiple components.[55] In tracing change from the "traditional" to the "modern" set we cannot assume that all elements change together. This is recognized by Kahl as indicated by his preference for attitude profiles based on multi-continua of modernity. But the very multiplicity of profiles brings the conceptual usefulness of "modern man" into doubt. Nonetheless, the components of modern man proposed by these would apparently live in a humane, urban, and utopian democracy.[56] But merely living there is not sufficient to make one modern, for he argues " ... it is only when man has undergone a change in spirit—has acquired certain new ways of thinking, feeling, and acting—that we come to consider him truly modern."[57] The society apparently becomes "modern" first, and after some lag creates modern man.

The society's level of development would thus determine the frequency of "moderns." Modern men, therefore, are a product, not the cause, of growth. But Inkeles concedes that modern qualities can be found among habitants of less affluent environments[58] and were present, for example, among the ancient Greeks and Elizabethan English. He apparently therefore vacillates between a view of an ideal-typical future man and a concept of timeless rational man. His elements of modernity, however, are designed to apply to people in contemporary underdeveloped societies. The implication is that cultivating these qualities will help the countries develop economically, politically, and socially.

The elements are assumed to hold together—changes along the dimension of one being accompanied by congruent changes in the others—as "relatively coherent factors"[59] (in the statistical sense). For the individual, modernity is a *gestalt*. Its elements may be summarized as follows:[60]

(1) *Readiness for change.* This is a "psychological disposition" that makes new experience and change acceptable to the individual. It appears to be closely bound to structural changes that have influenced the individual in the past. Even sophisticated urban man is caught in the duality of desires for novelty and stability. Thus, contrary to Inkeles' evolutionary view, it may be possible for a wooden plow farmer to be more "ready" for change than a tractor driver.

(2) *Wide scope of opinions.* This is in part a function of communications systems. Inkeles adds that the individual is more modern if his opinions are "democratic." Communists and Fascists presumably reflect primordial sentiments.

(3) *Present and future orientation,* rather than a preoccupation with the past. In this he includes the ability to value time, keep to schedules, be punctual, and organize future activities.

(4) *Planning orientation*—a belief in organization and planning "as a way of life." Here, of course, leftist believers in planned economies score well.

(5) *Efficacy*—a belief in man's ability to "dominate" his environment to his own ends. It is unclear how the ecological prophets-of-doom would score here.

(6) *Calculability*—a belief that the world is knowable and predictable, and confidence "that other people and institutions around him

can be relied upon to fulfill or meet their obligations and responsibilities." This is clearly tied to structural conditions: Anyone who holds this view under conditions of a reign of terror, or instantaneous law and corruption, is not "modern" but sociopathic.

(7) *Dignity* —an awareness of the "natural rights" of others. Inkeles refers specifically to those of women and children. He wants equalitarian family patterns.

(8) *Faith in science and technology* —but surely he cannot mean a blind faith. It is hard to believe in new technology when, for example, it takes away one's livelihood, kills one's family, or destroys the environment.

(9) *Distributive justice* —"rewards should be according to contribution," not ascriptive. But what constitutes justice is not a universal natural law, but a matter for social definition.

Inkeles' elements are seen to be largely dependent on social structure. They are the idealized aspects and products of modern industrial societies. As such, they cannot be linked directly to the economic growth of national economies.

Kahl's concept of modern man is descriptive. Using questionnaire data from Brazil and Mexico on fourteen hypothesized "modern" dimensions, he devised (by factor analysis) seven that empirically go together.

> A modern man is an activist; he attempts to shape his world instead of passively and fatalistically responding to it. He is an individualist, who does not merge his work career with that of either relatives or friends. He believes that an independent career is not only desirable but possible for he perceives both life chances and the local community to be low in ascribed status. He prefers urban life to rural life, and he follows the mass media.[61]

He found that the degree of modernism depended in part on the subject's place of residence (urban as opposed to rural), but more strongly on his social status. When these two variables were controlled, the similarities between Brazilians, Mexicans, and North Americans were great. Kahl therefore concludes that "position in the social structure determines the degree of modernism, and nationality differences are not important."[62] Neither, we may deduce, are economic levels (as measured by per capita Gross National Product) and growth rates since these vary greatly for the countries in Kahl's study. Modern man, it appears, is not necessarily developmental man. We must look elsewhere for individual traits which, given a set of as yet unspecified conditions, will foster economic growth.

NOTES

1. George A. Theodorson, "Industrialization and Urbanization," in J. L. Finkle and R. W. Gable (eds.), *Political Development and Social Change* (New York: John Wiley & Sons, 1966), p. 297.
2. Clark Kerr, J. T. Dunlop, F. H. Harbison, and C. A. Myers, *Industrialism and Industrial Man* (New York: Oxford University Press, 1964), pp. 17-18.
3. See Herbert Blumer, "Early Industrialization and the Laboring Class," in *Sociological Quarterly*, vol. I, no. 1 (Jan., 1960), pp. 5-14.
4. For example, Bendix has shown the importance of preindustrial ideologies in Russia and England: In the former, historical legacies prevented the shift in ideology that took place in England, and industrial authority remained paternalistic. Thus, although an "ethnic of work performance" was demanded by the industrial process, it was shaped by traditional factors. See R. Bendix, *Work and Authority in Industry* (New York: Harper Torchbooks, 1963), especially pp. 435-445.
5. Clifford Geertz, *Peddlers and Princes* (Chicago: University of Chicago Press, 1963), p. 263.
6. Milton Singer, "Changing Craft Traditions in India," in W. E. Moore and A. S. Feldman (eds.), *Labor Commitment and Social Change in Developing Areas* (New York: Social Science Research Council, 1960), p. 263.
7. This is a recurrent theme among critics of development theory. For a recent and thoughtful example, see Paul Streeten, "Critique of Development Concepts," *European Journal of Sociology,* vol. XI, no. 1, 1970, pp. 67-80.
8. Manning Nash, "Social Aspects of Economic Development," in Finkle and Gable, *op. cit.,* p. 286.
9. See H. Blumer, "The Idea of Social Development," *Studies in Comparative International Development,* vol. II, no. 1 (1966). For a discussion of this article and an argument for the usefulness of a reconstructed concept of social development, see Manfred Stanley, "Social Development as a Normative Concept," *Journal of Developing Areas,* April, 1967, pp. 301-316.
10. S. N. Eisenstadt, "Problems of Integration and Modernization Breakdowns," in Finkle and Gable, *op. cit.,* p. 575.
11. S. N. Eisenstadt, *Modernization: Protest and Change* (Englewood Cliffs, N.J.: Prentice-Hall, 1966).
12. R. Bendix, *Nation Building and Citizenship: Studies of Our Changing Social Order* (New York: John Wiley & Sons, 1964), p. 5.
13. *Ibid.,* p. 299.
14. Wilbert E. Moore, *The Impact of Industry* (Englewood Cliffs, N.J.: Prentice-Hall, 1965), p. 16.
15. *Ibid.,* p. 4.
16. *Ibid.,* p. 5.
17. *Ibid.,* p. 6.
18. Marion Levy, *Modernization and the Structure of Societies,* vol. I (Princeton: Princeton University Press, 1966).
19. *Ibid.,* p. 90.
20. David Apter, *The Politics of Modernization* (Chicago: University of Chicago Press, 1965), p. 43.

21. *Ibid.,* p. 43.
22. *Ibid.,* p. 57.
23. *Ibid.,* p. 68.
24. *Ibid.,* p. 67.
25. I. L. Horowitz, *Three Worlds of Development* (New York: Oxford University Press, 1966), p. 306.
26. This is the more accurate term to describe the process of unification within many extremely heterogeneous "new nations." Their problem is not that of subduing feudal barons, but of forging one single culture from radically different ones. I am indebted to Dr. Guenther Roth for drawing my attention to the term, and the distinctness of its referent. See his article "Personal Rulership, Patrimonialism, and Empire-Building in the New States," *World Politics,* vol. XX, no. 2, January, 1968, pp. 194-206
27. See Irving L. Horowitz, "The Norm of Illegitimacy," *Soundings,* vol. LI, no. 1 (Spring, 1968).
28. Gino Germani, "Social Change and Intergroup Conflicts," in Irving L. Horowitz (ed.), *The New Sociology* (New York: Oxford University Press, 1964), pp. 399-400.
29. *Ibid.,* p. 402.
30. Gino Germani, "Mass Immigration and Modernization in Argentina," *Studies in Comparative International Development,* vol. II, no. 11, 1966.
31. See, for example, Cyril E. Black, *The Dynamics of Modernization* (New York: Harper and Row, 1966).
32. Empirically minded social scientists have used existing concepts but only at the cost of crude assignment of indicators and naïve assumptions of theoretical and conceptual unanimity among "theorists."
33. The first term, "breakdown," was suggested by S. N. Eisenstadt, *op. cit.,* 1964, discussed above. The latter two are proposed by Ian Weinberg, *The Concept of Modernization: An Unfinished Chapter in Sociological Theory* (University of Toronto, February, 1969 [mimeo], draft of a paper read at the ASA Annual Meeting, Boston, August, 1968). While questioning the monolithic nature of the concept, Weinberg did not reject it.
34. Morris E. Opler has stressed that a recognition of man's potential to shape his culture is necessary if *positive* contributions to developmental change are sought. See his "Developmental Change and the Nature of Man," in Gallaher, *op. cit.,* pp. 17-35.
35. D. C. McClelland, *The Achieving Society* (Princeton: Van Nostrand, 1961).
36. See his article "The Impulse to Modernization," in Myron Weiner (ed.), *Modernization: The Dynamics of Growth* (New York: Basic Books, 1966).
37. In a more recent work, McClelland gives some attention to differential opportunities and innovative behavior and cites cases where lack of the former has inhibited the yield due to a high nAch. He points out that perception of opportunities rather than the opportunities themselves is the crucial factor. But he fails to answer previous criticism relating to the lack in his theory of any consideration for the structural constraints on opportunity. Neither, it seems, is it conceivable that some economic behavior that is sound for the individual might be damaging for the community or society as a whole. See D. C. McClelland and D. G. Winter, *Motivating Economic Achievement* (New York: Free Press, 1969), especially pp. 15-25.
38. R. A. LeVine, *Dreams and Deeds* (Chicago: University of Chicago Press, 1966).
39. *Ibid.,* p. 3. Another observer of the African scene notes the widespread cupidity of the urban African, who is well motivated by material rewards even though they can be attained only by corrupt means. See S. Andreski, *The African Predicament* (New York: Atherton, 1969).
40. Everett E. Hagen, *On the Theory of Social Change* (Homewood, Ill.: Dorsey, 1962).
41. Max Weber, *The Protestant Ethic and the Spirit of Capitalism,* trans. by Talcott Parsons (New York: Charles Scribner's Sons, 1958).
42. Kurt Samuelson, *Religion and Economic Action: A Critique of Max Weber* (New York: Harper Torchbooks, 1961). For a full examination of the Protestant Ethic, see S. N. Eisenstadt (ed.), *The Protestant Ethic and Modernization* (New York: Basic Books, 1968).

43. S. M. Lipset, "Values, Education, and Entrepreneurship," in Lipset and Solari (eds.), *op. cit.,* pp. 3-60.
44. Fernando H. Cardoso, "The Entrepreneurial Elites of Latin America," *Studies in Comparative International Development,* vol. 2, no. 10, 1966, p. 147.
45. F. H. Cardoso, "The Industrial Elite," in Lipset and Solari (eds.), *op. cit.,* pp. 94-114.
46. François Bourricaud, "Structure and Function of Peruvian Oligarchy, *Studies in Comparative International Development,* vol. II, no. 2, 1966.
47. Luis Ratinoff, "The New Urban Groups: The Middle Classes," in Lipset and Solari (eds.), *op. cit.,* pp. 61-93.
48. Andrew G. Frank, "Urban Poverty in Latin America," *Studies in Comparative International Development,* vol. II, no. 5, 1966.
49. D. Lerner et al., *The Passing of Traditional Society* (New York: Free Press, 1958).
50. *Ibid.,* p. 326.
51. *Ibid.,* p. 231.
52. *Ibid.,* p. 13.
53. A. Inkeles, "The Modernization of Man," in Weiner, *op. cit.,* pp. 138-145.
54. J. A. Kahl, *The Measurement of Modernism* (Austin: University of Texas Press, 1968).
55. For a recent critique of "modernity" and a demonstration of its non-unidimensionality, see Allan Schnaiberg, "Measuring Modernism: Theoretical and Empirical Explorations," *American Journal of Sociology,* vol. 76, no. 3 (November, 1970), pp. 399-425.
56. Inkeles, *op. cit.,* p. 138.
57. *Ibid.,* p. 140.
58. *Ibid.,* p. 143.
59. *Ibid.,* p. 141.
60. *Ibid.,* pp. 141-144.
61. Kahl, *op. cit.,* p. 37.
62. *Ibid.,* p. 21.

3.

an alternate approach: consumerism, producerism, and development theory

The aim of this chapter is to develop intermediate concepts between the prevailing opposites currently in use. For want of a better term, these may be called "analytical concepts." They should be general enough to cover "big" events and clusters of social happenings, but also be viable at "micro" or individual levels. Thus unlike the overlapping macro formations of the grand theorists (including many of the Titans of old), they should be mutually exclusive and far more amenable to empirical referents than the usual ephemeral *zeitgeists*. On the other hand they should be more "whole" intellectually than the neatly intercorrelated indices that the raw empiricists offer us. The researchers may of course claim that their measures are indicators for some theoretical referent, but the validity of the indicator, which is of course always open to doubt, is more tenuous than in other more limited areas of sociology. This is because of the extreme abstract-

40

ness of the original concepts in studies of development. Indeed in some work we have an interchangeability of concepts[1] rather than of indicators as called for by the survey research tradition.

The concepts suggested here, of course, will have some of the disadvantages of existing concepts. But they should be closer to empirical reality than current "grand" theory formulations, and have more meaning than the empiricists' inductive factors. The object here is not to produce immediately measurable concepts, but simpler and more useful heuristic (or sensitizing) ones that link economic, psychological, and social variables.[2]

OUTLINE OF MAJOR CONCEPTS

Development

At least when compared to the sociologists' definition, the economists' use of the term is a reasonably concrete macro concept for which reasonable dimensions and indicators, if not precise measures, such as growth rates in Gross National Product and per capita income, are readily available. Political scientists and sociologists have been less successful. "Political development" and "political modernization" are seldom clarified at the conceptual level even though concrete "indicators" for them have been widely used. They apparently serve to obscure less universal but more concrete concepts such as democratization and political centralization, and tacitly assume that these latter two processes accompany—in some cases are even functional to—economic development. "Social development," as Blumer[3] has noted, is vaguer still. If what is meant is nation-building, institutional centralization, or enhanced social control—which themselves are by no means simple, unambiguous concepts—then those terms should surely be used, not hidden in the metaphysics of "social development." The seeming equality with economists in the development field that we derive by using this parallel term is perhaps more of a surface and semantic parity. The term itself is less useful analytically; rather it is a general rubric, vaguely defined, under which the sociologist groups many social processes that are not necessarily interrelated.

The use of "social development" may be dangerous if it is interpreted as a pejorative term which implies that "developed" countries are socially "better" than underdeveloped ones. In fact, social life may be more intense, if less extended, in the latter.

Searches for community and for intimacy are phenomena of developed societies; it is these societies, evidently, that lack meaningful primary relationships. When it means the extension of organized social services, social development may be a useful concept, but it is misnamed. It could be more appropriately labeled as "social security" or "welfare development."

Development of the economic variety is more apt to be researchable and valid. Moreover, it is a viable challenge to the sociologist who would explain it in social terms. Several notable sociologists of the past (for example, Weber, Marx, Veblen) did not hesitate to employ concepts from other disciplines. Indeed, their interdisciplinary work makes their classification under present academic headings a difficult task. Many social scientists are returning to what must now be called a "multidisciplinary approach." In line with this trend, my dependent variable is economic in conception. But since definitions of economic development are not unanimously accepted and because they are usually more concerned with the measurement than the idea of development, a more abstract view of material growth is taken here. Accordingly, *development* is defined in this study as the *sustained growth of material output of a society if such ouput adds to the total material wealth.* It should be noted that producing ten million automobiles per annum does not increase the total workable autos by this amount—the total is dependent on the quality of existing vehicles, both their durability and the life-span of their aesthetic appeal. Clearly, increases in the production of some goods (for example, machine tools) will induce greater direct growth in the immediate future than others (for example, children's toys).

My definition is concerned with increases in the national wealth of nations. As such, this is closer to Colin Clark's economic welfare definition than Paul Baran's "per capita output of material goods."[4] The latter would be closer to a measure of what I would call "producerism." Growth in total wealth cannot be directly *measured,* but the familiar data of economists—Gross National Product, GNP per capita and output figures—can be utilized to *indicate* rates of accumulation. Such measures, of course, assume that the social value of products is reflected by their market prices, an assumption that few economists would rigidly hold.[5] Even if we ignore the possibility that advertising may induce changes in consumer preference that do not enhance individual welfare, the switch from "traditional" to more sophisticated industrial goods, even though it produces an increase in national accounting figures, should not be simplistically assumed to increase *public* welfare. In addition, GNP figures may include services not reported previously or in other countries (for example, the sudden inclusion of house- wives' services in GNP accounting would enhance the indicated growth rate, but the actual increase in wealth would be overesti- mated), and per capita figures compound actual growth in wealth and population. Standard economic data are therefore only indica- tors, not measures, of the concept of development used here.

Consumerism

This concept is based on elements often included in definitions of modernization.[6] As used here, *consumerism* means the *increase in consumption of the material culture of the developed countries.* It embraces the local manufacture and marketing, as well as the impor- tation, of modern consumer goods prevalent in rich-country markets—household durables, automobiles, and fashionable products for the body and home. The production of these goods usually requires sophisticated, non-labor intensive, technology. Final market- ing demands advanced packaging, considerable product differentia- tion, and the exhortations of advertising that are necessary to induce consumer demand.

The widespread desire to participate in this "modern" material culture is apparently induced by the mass madia, and by direct emulation of those who have been able to translate their desires into actual participation. Galbraith, for example, has pointed out that

> Considerable extremes of wealth and income continue to exist in nearly all of the less developed lands. These can create a strong drag on demand in the direction of higher-priced or luxury products. And this tendency is especially insidious for many of these products are commonplace in the standard of living of the more advanced countries and equally so, and for that reason, in the consumption habits of the upper-income minority of the poorer country. To the extent that high incomes of the minority draw development resources into privileged consumption, social differences are widened and to the strains associated with poverty may be added those associated with obvious differences in well-

being. People may come to sense that economic development is
not for the many but for the few.[7]

Most underdeveloped countries have a segment of the population
that is able to live in such a modern "cosmopolitan" material
world, which contrasts markedly with the larger "transitional"
segment. I shall call this phenomenon of uneven material development "sectorism."[8] It is closely connected with consumerism.

Consumerism is a social concept, the outcome of social and
interpersonal influences. It is encouraged in much of the Third
World by Western commercial pressures. The United States and
Europe are happy to trade (or dump) their "surplus" consumer
goods, and where permitted, will launch advertising drives to
achieve their purpose. The high consumption abroad of Hollywood
films and other Western-dominated mass communications (for
example, radio, TV, and printed advertising) also helps to induce
needs for "modern" products. Although only an elite few can
actually consume in the Western manner, the desire to do so is
widespread, both because of these outside influences and in
imitation of the Westernized domestic elite. Much import substitution should therefore be seen as a corollary of consumerism rather
than of industrialization, since it is designed to maintain and
increase this type of domestic consumption.

Consumerism may be charged with having an anti-Western bias,
but this is not the intention. It merely points to the existence of
widespread and growing consumption patterns that spread from the
rich countries to the poor. As such, it is a concept that focuses
attention on the world context of development, on the external
influences that are brought to bear on "developing" countries.

Consumerism sets up demands for "modern" goods both at the
retail and at the institutional levels. The latter may be composed
of the growth of prestige-oriented public works (deluxe school
buildings, libraries, government offices, etc.)—what Galbraith calls
"Symbolic Modernization"[9]—and the development of modern but
"unproductive bureaucracies and even more expensive and no less
redundant military establishments."[10] To make application of the
concept to empirical cases simpler, however, I shall focus on only
the private (or retail) forms of consumerism. The public forms will
therefore be ignored here, not because they are unimportant, but
because they introduce too much complexity.

Producerism

This concept denotes the *increased mobilization of a society's population to work, and to work more productively in the non-consumerist sector of the economy.* Producerism should raise the total production of standardized goods that meet the basic housing, clothing, and food needs of the *mass* population, in addition to generating saving for reinvestment in the mass sector. The consumption of such goods is in fact itself a form of investment since it upgrades the working capacity of those who enjoy them. Social organization and mobilization are the keys to producerism as conceived here. Thus, if peasants work more days per year and agricultural production per acre per man thereby increases, this will be taken as an example of producerism.

Improved skills and tools (what is usually called "industrialization") are important factors in adding to the social product. But the increase of "modern" machinery rather than basic production tools—cheap power sources, hand tools, and simple plant—does not necessarily indicate optimum society-wide producerism. Such, for example, is the case with the low labor utilizing equipment[11] that characterizes consumerism. The importation of tractors by local landowners—or donated as foreign aid—may have an advantageous economic effect for the *landowner.* It reduces his labor costs and at the same time may increase productivity. The labor so displaced, however, may still incur costs to the society.[12] The workers do not become what Eisenstadt[13] has called "free-floating resources"—by which he means mobile innovating forces—they become society's flotsam and add to the existing pool of unproductive labor. The cost of the tractor is also borne by society in the form of a weakened foreign exchange position, which continues after the initial capital outlay due to the cost of necessary replacement parts. Even the increased economic value yielded to the landowner is often lost by his overseas investment in, for example, the New York Stock Exchange or Swiss banks. Certainly, then, mechanization of agriculture may mean that fewer people are being mobilized for production in the mass sector, and therefore producerism as I have defined it cannot be assumed, indeed it may be retarded.

Producerism may be seen to have two main dimensions: *material,* which involves the improvement of production implements and their wider distribution; and *human,* the improvement of productive skills, time spent in productive activity, and more efficient organization for work. It is an abstract concept of much larger scope than consumerism. Although it cannot be directly measured, potential indicators for this definition of producerism can be suggested. These include rates of growth in productivity, particularly in the secondary, but also in the primary, sector; increases in the quality of mass products, which may in part be measured by their durability (for example, of housing) and sale-ability on the domestic market; and the proportion of the working age population actively employed in non-subsistence occupations. Another valuable indicator—with the reservations about con-sumerist production expressed above—is the absolute growth of the secondary sector in terms of both capital plant and employment.

The instrumental capacity[14] of a society, broadly conceived, is perhaps a good backdrop from which to view producerism. This is a static concept, used here in the sense of the society's aggregate potential to mobilize productive activity. It includes the size of the population and its age structure, the skills of this population, its organizations and institutions, and its existing stock of natural resources and productive hardware. To facilitate producerism the society can (1) upgrade the portion of this capacity currently in use and/or (2) use an increasingly greater portion of the potential.

In the rich countries, developmental efforts center about the first. That is, attempts are made both to mechanize and to upgrade skills and spread them to more of the employed population. Economic planners will often draw on this experience and urge similar methods in poor countries. Along these lines, for example, it has been argued that ". . . the observed three-fold increase in the volume of goods and services produced (in Mexico) between 1940 and 1955 could have been accomplished with no increases in the total number of workers."[15] In fact, there was an increase in the "marginal" employment. This indicates that it is possible to adopt a different strategy for effecting producerism, one perhaps better suited to poor countries. This involves increasing the utilization of the society's total productive capacity. It can be done by employ-ing the unemployed and what were hitherto considered as the unemployable segments of the population—its women, youths, the aged; by lengthening the work hours per year of the employed, which implies a reduction of what is usually termed "underemploy-ment"; and by increasing the use of existing plant. For example, there is no real shortage of tractors and factory plant when the former stand idle during many hours of the harvest season, or when the latter is only used eight or twelve hours a day, 250 days per year.[16]

THE RELATIONSHIP OF PRODUCERISM AND CONSUMERISM TO DEVELOPMENT

Contrary to assumptions that economic growth is dependent upon the stage of growth already achieved, empirical evidence suggests that development is the outcome of dynamics of more limited timespan, perhaps more the product of day-to-day actions than of historical legacies and past accomplishments. Despite the elegance of stage theories,[17] examination of crude cross-national data for non-Communist nations, both rich and poor, indicates that development stages are not readily descernible. On the contrary, the data apparently supports the claims to autonomy. Among the poorer countries especially, a wide range of growth rates seems possible, at least in the short run (see Diagram 2). There is a wide variation between growth rates at all economic levels. When the countries in Diagram 2 are grouped into low and high groups on both growth rate and level, the relationship is weak and the reverse of that expected (see Table I, located at end of book). This was also found by Banks and Textor using a larger sample of countries: The poorer countries were overrepresented in a rapid growing category (Table II). From both sources of data the conclusion is therefore the same: It is apparently no more difficult for a poor country to grow rapidly than it is for a rich country to do so—indeed it may be easier.

I concur with Baran that the allocation of economic surplus is the key to development,[18] and that optimum development requires a "full utilization of all available productive resources."[19] In my own terms, development requires the maximization of producerism. Baran distinguishes between actual and potential surpluses in agriculture. The potential surplus, he claims, is lost in non-productive activities, among which he cites money lending and further land purchase; while actual surpluses are lost to the society by their use for overseas remittances and "luxury urban living,"[20] to which may be added the establishment of high import content

industries. In my terms, development lags because producerism—
the primary source of internal growth and of exports—is low, while
consumerism grows rapidly until it is checked by lack of export
earnings. It is the mix between consumerism and producerism[21]
that in part determines the usable economic surplus in society and
shapes its allocation.

Stage theories and notions about meeting the prerequisites of
economic take-off are therefore rejected here. Instead, consumerism is viewed as being basically antithetical to development (see
"Excess Consumerism and the Modern Sectors," section below),
while producerism promotes it. The relationship is illustrated by
the following typology of societies. The placement of actual
countries is, of course, subject to empirical determination. The
typology is formed by the artificial dichotomy of the two independent variables, and cross tabulating them to yield four hypothetical types of societies (see Diagram 3).

Type 1 is called "overdeveloped," and approximates the use of
the term by C.W. Mills and I.L. Horowitz. Here we have the mass
consumption economies, the modern West with the possible inclusion of Russia, Eastern Europe, and Japan. These countries do not
fully match the pure type. Built-in rates of economic growth are
relatively low due to widespread consumer demands; all economic
sectors, except the defense industries of the Big Two, grow at a
fairly sedate pace. Of the major countries, Britain is perhaps the
closest to the economic balance, if not in fact falling in Type 2.
Such economies are the field for Keynesian policies of induced
demand and the maintenance of consumer spending potential; and
by built-in obsolescence, they are the stage for the constant
redefinition (in material terms) of cosmopolitan consumer tastes.

Type 2 is the impasse situation of much of the Third World,
including most of Latin America. Due to the drive for instant
consumerism, development is very uneven, with the "modern"
sector[22] often having an exploitative relationship to the rest of the
society (subsistence sectors, at least theoretically, may be totally
isolated). Consumer values are instilled in the "have-nots," while
productive resources in the "modern" consumerist sector are
insufficient to meet their demands, and resources are diverted from
the manufacture of more feasible mass products. Echavarria has
outlined this situation well. He comments on current economic
"creeds" in Latin America as follows:

> The most striking internal contradiction in these creeds con-
> sists . . . in the fact that the desire for an improvement in the level
> of living or in consumer capacity may be unaccompanied by the
> parallel impulse to make the necessary effort to obtain it.[23]

Individual needs, he continues, are not held in check by individual
or collective responsibility. This, in addition to economic stagnation, is the ever present political problem of containing the
materialism of the "modernized"—albeit not revolutionary or productive—masses.

The relative size of the service sector in Type 2 countries is
often proportionately larger than that found in the "overdeveloped" countries. As Landsberger[24] has noted, in the latter type the
ratio of employment in the secondary (manufacturing) sector to
that in the tertiary (or service) sector is normally around 1:1, and
may be as low as 1:½. But in Latin America, which he argues
plausibly cannot afford it, the ratio is much higher. In Chile it is
1:1.3, in Honduras 1:2. Clearly the service sectors are disproportionately large. This situation is tolerable only if the primary
sector can sustain the continually growing demands placed upon it.
Empirical evidence suggests that this is not the case in most
unevenly "modernized" undeveloped countries, for they cannot
adequately finance internal consumption and investment needs.

In *Type 3,* "developing societies," urges to consumerism are denied
or absent while the society's emphasis is on producerism—the
mobilization of effort to fulfill the basis needs of the population.
Savings can be "ploughed back" into the "mass" sector, rather
than used to underwrite a consumerist enclave. Countries placed
hypothetically in this type include the Western capitalist countries
in their rapid growth stages (through largely self-imposed individu-
alist restraints and widespread ignorance and indeed relative
absence of cosmopolitan styles) and some of the communist
countries (through elite domination of the masses). It is probably
to an elite model, but not necessarily a communist one, that one
must look for future transformation of societies into this type,
since it is perhaps unrealistic to expect voluntary individual
suppression of consumerism in the face of international commercial
pressures. Historically, nationalism has been a valuable device for
muting consumer drives and promoting indigenous industry. The
latter perhaps is a paradoxical aim of nationalism since technology

is usually borrowed from other nations. Clearly, then, this type of nationalism is a modern phenomenon, not a return to some kind of folk traditionalism. By this method such countries as economically disparate as Japan, Russia, China, and the United States (in its isolationist, and by European standards "culturally" philistine, stage) have suppressed earlier, less virulent forms of consumerism, or rather redefined it in terms that their economies could handle. Among the newly independent states, the Tanzanian government is apparently attempting long-range development in this way. Cuba, not entirely of its own volition, has broken away from consumerist dualism, and Japan appears to have been selective in the choice of consumerist elements and the timing of their adoption from the outset of its industrialization. Other developing countries, for example, those that base their policies on anti-imperialism (if by this they mean anti-"luxury" consumer goods), will probably follow this mode of development.

Several countries that are now of Type 2 have, of course, had a rapid development period. Horowitz has pointed out that despite the seemingly unsuitable mass psychology in Latin America, its "comparative decline . . . with respect to North America is directly and proportionately related to the heavy scale North European and North American capital investments in the region."[25] External exploitation effects cannot of course be dismissed, but the internal effects were perhaps more thoroughgoing: The seeds of consumerism were no doubt planted, and the need for internal exploitation to support the indigenous but modernist colony follows logically.

Type 4 is the truly "undeveloped" type with relatively stagnant productivity among the masses and a traditional elite, if any, uninfluenced by international consumer styles. Perhaps Tibet, before it was re-absorbed as a Chinese province, and other isolationist countries of the past (such as the Boer Republic) best approximate this type. Contemporary Paraguay, Albania, and Haiti may be today's closest counterparts. Isolated peasant groups in parts of the Third World may appear to be of this type, but their society as a whole usually falls in either Type 2 or 3. Outside influences, if anything, tend to induce consumerism before the more sophisticated economic and political drive to producerism can get under way.

This typology of societies is based primarily on material factors. This is not to say that rich, growing nations are necessarily "good" societies, nor that cultural and social goals should be dominated by entirely economic ones. Rather, what is attempted here is to uncover the fundamental processes which, for better or for worse, lead to greater material wealth. Although openly materialistic philosophies are rightly unfashionable among the affluent people in the overdeveloped countries, it should be remembered that "the wretched of the earth"[26] may be far more concerned with a share of material goods. But clearly the object of producerism is not only the creation of wealth (development), but also the use of such wealth. Thus mass consumption, including perhaps that of a few "modern" goods, is one of its objectives. The complete absence of consumerism might therefore be detrimental to both producerism and development. If consumerism grows much faster than producerism, however, the sectoral nature of the economy is heightened and development is impaired. This results because investments that would stimulate future producerism are sacrificed for modern sector consumption. In addition, new investments may deemphasize labor intensive organization by stressing sophisticated import substitution products. Although these reduce the immediate demands for foreign exchange, the need for machinery replacements and often raw materials ensures that it is not altogether eliminated.

CONSUMERISM, PRODUCERISM, AND DEVELOPMENTAL MAN

In Chapter 2 it was noted that current theories of development generally focus on either the "macro" phenomena in societies or the individual psychologies of their members. The former neglects voluntary human behavior, the latter the effects of social structures on individuals. In consequence, rather than complementing each other, the theories at the two levels of analysis are more frequently conflicting views or interpretations of events in society. It is claimed here that the concepts of producerism and consumerism (and the theory of development built from them) are more amenable to use at the micro level than the standard macro concepts, industrialization and modernization. As such, they are useful tools in breaking down the "abstractness" of development theorizing, and forging a theory that takes into account the interdependence of man and society.

It was argued in the previous chapter that when Inkeles and Kahl described the characteristics of "modern" man, they were outlining the type best suited for complex industrial societies. The elements and items that compose their definitions of modernity were seen to be the result of adaptations to individually experienced modern conditions. That moderns are to be found in Mexico and Brazil indicates that there is a modern sector, not that these countries as a whole are modern, industrial, or developing. Economic growth rates in the developed countries are not as high as those needed by countries wishing to catch up, and the growth they generate is probably due more to technological than basic character changes. Developmental man—the type that enhances growth—is not the same as "modern" man; nor, as has been shown, can he be a Victorian entrepreneur and survive in a world of international enterprise.

It has been claimed that in the case of many of the "underdeveloped" countries, it has been relatively easy to build a modern parasitic sector in the economy, and transmit information of Western consumer styles. This inevitably shapes the attitudes and consumption patterns of both masses and elites in a way that inhibits development. The degree of consumerism and producerism at the societal level should be reflected in individuals by their shaping of two parallel attitude sets. A typology of developmental attitude types can therefore be constructed. It will be noted that this resembles my typology of societies. Individuals in each of these societies, however, may have any of the four possible attitude sets. The attitude types and sets are first described, and then the relevance of the distribution of the types in a society to its economic growth is considered.

Developmental attitudes. Development has been described in part as the product of the interplay between the processes of consumerism and producerism. A developmental attitude set is taken to be the corresponding mix of consumer and producer attitudes. The highly developmental set can be equated with Weber's "spirit of capitalism," which is a special case, or with Mills' description of the capitalist type of industrial man:

. . . a man who has material gain uppermost: who is individuated—no guilt or anxiety is experienced if he "gets ahead"; in fact he feels guilt if he does not. He is disciplined for work, which means that he spends the most alert hours of the best days of his life working. He is sober and calculating, and in that sense rational.[27]

Where development stemmed from elite domination, the values of the leadership were essentially the same. Mills' communist type, for example, also has a "puritanical strain,—[for] he too glorified work, in his case of a collective sort."[28] In both of these definitions there appear to be two crucial elements: motivation to work, and a reluctance to consume the products of this work—the ascetic element, or negation of "modernity." If the asceticism involves the rejection of cosmopolitan consumer durables, and work emphasis means effort in the mass market of unsophisticated necessities, these elements correspond closely to a "micro" application of consumerism and producerism.

Producer attitudes are defined as the work and productivity drives in the individual that are geared to basic sectors of the economy. They are a more specific variety—that is, the ends of the activity are cited—of what McClelland has called the "achievement motive" in economic development when this term is also stripped of its entrepreneurial connotations. The wide distribution of producer attitudes, particularly on the mass level, but also among strategically placed members of society, will facilitate producerism (as I have defined it). Echavarria has described in a slightly more general way (he includes productivity in the consumerist occupations) what is meant here. He talks of a "capacity for execution and achievement— that is, the capacity for work in the broadest sense of the term."[29] These attitudes, it should be noted, are often considered components in definitions of "modernism." They should, it is maintained, be conceptualized separately.

Consumer attitudes are also present in most of the Third World. Basically these are consumption drives shaped by the continually changing standards of rich countries. That is, the desire for "modern" sophisticated products, including perhaps imported cars, Hollywood pools, washing machines (where human counterparts are plentiful and cheap), stereo records, and imposing buildings. These desires are apparently easy to induce as Lerner's already cited field work and the observations of many casual observers well demonstrate. For example, according to Landsberger,[30] the basic aims of Latin American labor are "mundane ones" and the urbanized workers in the "modern" sector are generally materialistic rather than revolutionary. Landsberger neither condemns nor condones these dominant values, but it will be shown that they are not a neutral factor in development.

Individual development types (derived from the concepts of consumer and producer attitude sets). The relative strength of the two sets determines the net developmental orientation of the individual. If each set of values is arbitrarily dichotomized into high and low categories, cross tabulation again yields four development types (see Diagram 4), which resemble the types in the "macro" level typology. These may be described as follows:

Type 1, "Hedonistic." This is perhaps becoming the dominant pattern in the West. The fruits of labor are to be consumed as soon as possible or even in advance, and production is geared to consumerist products. There is no place for any remnant of ascetic ideology. The tendency is to move toward Type 2—producerism declines in face of consumerism pressures. Thus craftsmanship and a desire for practical, low budget goods, is the declining value set.

Type 2, "Parasitic." In this type, modern goods are strongly desired, but the work ethic conducive to mass goods production is absent. It may closely characterize the Latin American Labor Unionists, "modern" elites in much of the Third World, and the peasant migrants to those urban centers which have a "modern" character. Previous quotations from Lerner demonstrate this set well enough. Mercier finds in Africa a similar acceptance of consumer modernity before productive skills in the basic industries have developed. He makes the following observations on the blacks in Dakar:

> Food remains a basic and traditional element in every category although certain European foods (bread, condensed milk, and preserves) have been adopted even by the least Europeanized. Only the categories of salaried employees and senior civil servants and of the liberal professions are found to have blended the two traditions more fully. The same tendency is observable with respect to the

material things of life: personal comfort, etc. For instance, new demands for furniture are everywhere in evidence, even among manual laborers.[31]

The developmental problem here is to get people to work more productively to achieve their basic demands, not to "awaken" them to modern consumer products.

Type 3, the "ascetic developmental." This is the set that must be possessed at least by the economic controllers if development is to take place. It may be called "self-sacrifice, altruism, dedication, purpose, and even divine madness,"[32] This was the ascetic type supposedly prevailing in the capitalism of the West in its "take-off" stage. It is difficult to instill because of the near impossibility of maintaining isolation from consumerism: How to keep the boys down on the farm (or at the lathe, or any productive task) for low rewards after they've seen Paris (or any great Western city of consumption—or even a Sears' catalogue) is an extremely difficult task.

Type 4, "Traditional." This is the rare attitude set exhibited by those as yet unaffected by the developed world. Material wants are unchanging and low, and work is viewed as a necessary evil or habitual way of life. Note that craftsmen, artists, and others in "traditional" societies do not follow this pattern; some "old rich" in the West, however, may do so. The latter are relatively unaffected by new advertising drives, and may have a leisure rather than a work ethic—even if their money is put to productive work. The disenchanted (but not the militant) poor in complex societies might also, perhaps, be categorized as this type.

Growing Economies. For the national economy to grow, it must be dominated by individuals who can act upon their ascetic attitude sets. (This set, of course, does not exhaust the total personality of the individual. We are not dealing with "modern man," but with a few important *aspects* of some contemporary men.) This means that either most men must be of this type; a good number must be extremely hard working, immune to seductive advertising, and ascetic; or the political economy must be dominated by them. Such an elite must hold in check the demands for consumerism within the society, especially of the "parasitic" personalities. They are also responsible for building the type of society that will nurture developing men of the future, for only those individuals with "developmental" personality sets, it is claimed, can do this.

EXCESS CONSUMERISM AND THE MODERN SECTORS

The focus of the study so far has been on the social factors that influence material development in the underdeveloped countries and regions. Material wealth, to be sure, should not be the only concern of the social scientist. Many have warned against such crass materialism and documented fully the shackles that advanced technology can impose.[33] But most national governments and their subjects want to increase their wealth themselves; the desire for material development is not a simple imposition of the "materialistic" rich countries. Europeans may sneer at the materialism of the United States, but at the same time strive to catch up; and Communists expect ultimately to show their superiority not just by building a new society and creating the new "socialist man," but by their superior ability to generate wealth. The peoples in the poorest countries are equally intent on emerging from their material wretchedness.

Modernization and industrialization are two concepts usually related to development in the literature. Examination of these two terms, however, showed that their meaning varies greatly from one writer to the next. Two elements usually enmeshed in these concepts were isolated and reconceptualized as consumerism and producerism. They were seen to operate at both societal and individual levels. Consumerism is claimed to be potentially detrimental to development, although other factors, which may mask its effect, may also influence the generation of wealth. For example, bonanza enterprises, such as oil and other extractive industries, may keep an economy growing irrespective of the population's consumer/producer balance, even if they accentuate sectorism.

Consumerism is the replication of developed country life styles in the "modern" sectors of underdeveloped countries. These sectors— usually having an urban locale—may range from outright satellites of foreign "industrial" economies to benign stimuli for local imaginations. But in the former and more common case the modern sector is clearly linked to the outside rather than to the countries' domestic economy. Baran has described this for an earlier epoch:

> Whatever market for manufactured goods emerged in the colonial and dependent countries did not become the "internal market" of these countries. Thrown wide open by colonization and by unequal treaties, it became an appendage of the "internal market" of Western capitalism.[34]

The form of international markets remains and apparently the Soviet bloc presents a similar satellitic scheme. Thus some consumerism is to be expected in all but totally isolated countries. It becomes excessive only when it runs beyond the utilized productive capacity of the society and grossly distorts economic priorities.

Severe sectoral imbalance in underdeveloped countries is widely recognized. But its existence alone is not proof that it is either necessary or desirable for effecting economic growth, even if government policies and scholarly recommendations would so assert. After a (static) factor analysis of non-communist poor countries, Adelman and Morris commit just this error in recommending policy.[35] In the poorest countries, they advise, emphasis should be on the modern market sector to intentionally increase dualism. The rationale here is presumably that this conforms to the past practices of the slightly richer countries. Only at intermediate levels, they argue, are industrialization and capital investment necessary; their object at this "stage" is to reduce "social tensions" by lessening imbalances and to "build the nation." It is not clear how industrialization can do either of these, for they are not advocating "intermediate technologies," but the "latest" sophisticated methods developed in the highly industrialized countries, that is, consumerism. Finally, to burst into "self- sustained growth," the richer underdeveloped countries need "economic modernization," a serious drive "for economic development supported by a reasonably competent committed leadership."

In addition to the fact that few of the low- and medium- level countries are actually capable of the type of long-range stage planning that Adelman and Morris propose, it is unclear why they could not go directly to the last stage, thereby avoiding the unnecessary dislocations of the first two. And to imply that the countries in this cross cultural study compose steps in a single evolutionary scheme, and thereby propose first establishing then disestablishing sectoral imbalances, assumes that these are both preconditions to growth. The former, it is claimed here, is not. The spectacular growth of such countries as Israel and Japan, and arguments already presented, suggest that internal dynamics rather than economic level determines whether or not growth is sustained. The producerism model of development was ignored by these two researchers, because prematurely "modern" and dualistic countries were predominant in their sample. Adelman and Morris conclude their recommendations by suggesting that the advanced countries should sell to the poor countries, but defer developmental aid and investment until the "stage" (if it ever comes) of "social tension" becomes irresistible; they are urging here the none too charitable policy that seems to be in effect already.

Two important social consequences of sectoral growth are frequently discussed in development literature; they are the related social phenomena, usually described under the rubrics of the "revolution of rising expectations" and the "demonstration effect." The former usually refers to rising mass needs for material goods. It was noted in Britain's early industrialization: "The universal discontent of men who felt themselves hungry in a society reeking with wealth, enslaved in a country which prided itself on its freedom, seeking bread and hope, and receiving in return stones and despair."[36] It was this basic dissonance between expectations and actual compensation that helped hold together the nascent labor movement. The same rising expectations and sense of injustice are claimed by many to be present among the black poor in the United States today. It characterizes the urbanized poor in the Third World. The "revolution" implies material needs and a politically expressed claim of a right to them. Without the latter there is merely an acceptance of inequality. Unfortunately, these rising expectations probably cannot be quenched, as Germani has claimed,[37] by merely integrating the poor into the social and political life of the "modern" sector; either a shift to truly mass-oriented production or the repression of the consumption demands made by the masses accompanied by continued sectorism are the more realistic options for dealing with the revolution.

The revolution of rising expectations stems from the politicalization of demands and from the cumulative presence of consumption in the modern sector—the demonstration effect. The consumption model displayed in the urban showplaces and in the life style of the elites (which is patterned after the developed country styles) is followed by the masses. There is a constant pressure for mass consumption of sophisticated goods (consumerism) that easily outstrips productive capacity and work orientations.[38] As has been shown, the labor movement in Latin America is not revolutionary in the ascetic Marxist sense. Instead, the unions together with the masses in general are pushing for the earliest possible enjoyment of bourgeois material comforts. For it is consumerism, not producerism, that the "effect" demonstrates to both elites and masses.

The social pressures for "modern" goods has directly affected economic priorities in the underdeveloped countries. The first effect of consumerism is a heavy reliance on consumer imports. These are usually paid for by the export of primary sector raw materials and easily processed foods. Due in part to the real or imagined downward trend of raw material prices relative to the price of manufactured goods (the thesis proposed by R. Prebisch of the U.N. Economic Commission for Latin America, or ECLA), a desire to gain international prestige, and a recognition that industrial countries are militarily powerful, most poor countries today attempt to increase their manufacturing capacity. The way they do this, and the selection of products, are often shaped by consumerism: Manufacture is by "modern" capital intensive means and the product is geared to replace sophisticated imported goods. The rationale for this is that earning more foreign exchange by expanding primary exports is more costly than cutting back on the import of finished goods by making them at home.[39]

The import substitution pattern of industrialization has far-ranging effects throughout the society. First, it does little to reduce sectoral imbalances—as Adelman and Morris assumed it would: Too few jobs are created, and output is not geared to the poorest half of the population. It has been estimated that in Latin America this lower part of the population accounted for only 9 per cent of the total sales of household consumer goods, and it was not effectively in the consumer durables market at all, while the top 5 per cent income group bought 74 per cent of the latter items.[40] Indigenous enterprises in underdeveloped countries can seldom afford the research and marketing overheads that permit the constant redefinition of consumer goods modernity in developed countries, since they lack both the scale and the resources of the modern international corporation. The target of modernity is a moving one that continually eludes the small operator. Thus trade barriers must be erected to protect the continuously "not-quite-the-latest" domestically made product from foreign competition. It is seldom successful on the world market.

The protected internal market may encourage too many enterprises in a given industry. In 1961, for example, 22 automotive firms were established in Argentina to serve a market requiring no more than 200,000 units per year.[41] Foreign corporations are usually interested in reentering the market from which they have been largely excluded by protectionism. They may be encouraged by the developing country's government to set up manufacturing plants locally so that research overheads are saved and recently patented products may be produced.

Both domestic and foreign enterprise in the underdeveloped country use the latest methods and machinery (which usually has to be imported), so their effect on the balance of trade is not entirely positive. The failure of both domestic and foreign enterprise to manufacture for export means that individually they incur an unfavorable balance with the outside world. The foreign company adds to this by persistent—albeit usually controlled—remittances to the "home" country. The growth and even the continued operation of the overseas branch is quite rationally the outcome of the parent company's needs, not those of the Third World country. As likely as not, the foreign corporation does not "substitute" for imports, but for goods already manufactured locally. With primary sectors that usually expand quite slowly, due in part to the emphasis on the "modern" sector, most countries that practice import substitution find themselves with periodic balance of payments crises that exist in the face of underutilized capacities of both manpower and plant.[42] Economic growth becomes dependent upon the capacity to import [43] rather than the success of indigenous saving and investment, the usual model proposed by economists who ignore international influences.[44] The *bête-noire* of development is therefore consumerism. The primary way in which it is introduced and maintained—through use of the mass media—will be evaluated in Chapter 4.

Implications of the Consumerism
Theory for the West

If the economic development of the Third World societies is really desired both by the leadership of these countries (when in fact, as everywhere else, they often exhibit strongly individualistic goals[45]) and by the United States[46] (whose short-run and perhaps also long-run *economic* interests are at stake), then certain conclusions may be drawn. From the theory of development proposed here, it is clear that consumerism must be downgraded. This is not, of course, to say it should be eliminated entirely, but that it should no longer be permitted to distort developing economies and perpetuate sectorism.

Assuming the West's desire to see these countries develop, a number of implications for foreign policy might be drawn. First, the policies of shoring up "modernist" regimes by military and economic aid are counter to such development, since these regimes perpetuate and exacerbate the sectorism that inhibits society-wide growth. Support should be given instead to nationalist ascetic leadership whenever it is present. It appears evident that Western corporate interests in these countries are not necessarily contiguous with long-term national Western interests. The impact, for example, of a corporation on a poor country's economy and its chances of developing can be very great. But the operation may be relatively unimportant to the corporation and even less so to its parent economy. And yet the lobbying power of the corporate interest in its home country is often much stronger than the poor nation's. Thus the rich nation's policies may be swayed to the long-term interests of neither country, but rather serve the short-term concerns of the highest bidder, the corporation.

It appears clear that culturally the developing countries need not, and indeed ultimately cannot, be "just like us." They can only be so in their producerism imperatives, in their desire to use their resources rationally in the interests of their populations. The appeals to variety and "quality" of Western goods in these countries are probably in large part spurious; that is, these products are not *in* their interests even if at the moment they are interested in such appeals.[47] Functionality of products should come first; the Western pattern of maximizing product appeal by packaging, advertising, and ephemeral surface dressing is perhaps a result of "saturated" market conditions and the productive systems in the rich countries. Neither condition pertains to the poor countries.

Since the spontaneous (individualistic) creation of producerism by the masses in Third World countries is unlikely (for they are already deeply imbued with "premature" consumerism), the use of coercion by a developmentalist elite is to be expected. With less hostility from outside to their development aims, their use of force may perhaps be more flexible and humane, but as successful as some earlier developmental elites. Such benign force would be less cruel, perhaps, than the disappointments and inequities that result from the hoax of premature modernization.

NOTES

1. Because the tertiary (or service) sector of economics is concentrated in urban areas, and forms part of a "middle class," its size has on occasion been used as an indicator for industrialization. It was used as such in a Chilean voting study and yielded evidence against the Marxian theory of increasing alienation (as measured by left-wing voting) with industrialization. Since the more obvious indicator for industrialization—per cent employed in manufacturing—showed no relationship to alienation, the adequacy of the tertiary index should have been doubted. The relationship found was perhaps between radical voting and modernization (or rather modernism—they were not dealing with *growth* of the sector), not industrialization. Deemphasis of concepts and indicator validity in order to maximize the interrelationships between indices is common in the hard data literature. The example cited here indicates that even sound researchers can err in this way. See G. Soares and R. L. Hamblin, "Socio-Economic Variables and Voting for the Radical Left: Chile, 1952," *American Political Science Review*, vol. LXI, no. 4, Dec., 1967, pp. 1058-1089.
2. William F. Whyte and Lawrence K. Williams among others have pointed to the need for such synthesis. See their *Toward an Integrated Theory of Development* (Ithaca: New York State School of Industrial and Labor Relations, Cornell University, ILR Paperback, no. 5, February, 1968, p. 81.
3. H. Blumer, "The Idea of Social Development," *Studies in Comparative International Development*, vol. II, no. I. This was discussed in more detail in the previous chapter.
4. See Paul A. Baran, *The Political Economy of Growth* (New York: Monthly Review Press, 1957), p. 18.
5. Many economists now question their colleagues' misplaced concreteness. This discrepancy between per capita output and its currency measures was brought to my attention by David Felix, *An Economist Looks at Modernization—With a Quizzical Eye*, Washington University, ([Mimeo], October 31, 1966).
6. "Political modernization" as a distinct concept usually means democratization, even though modern democracy predates totalitarian and perhaps even charismatic forms of government. My definition excludes the political dimensions of modernization.
7. J. K. Galbraith, *Economic Development* (Cambridge, Mass.: Harvard University Press, 1964), p. 7.
8. This phenomenon is of course widely recognized by observers of the Third World countries. In a recent work, for example, it was observed that industrial development in one of the most affluent of the "underdeveloped" countries, Chile, induced what is

clearly an example of sectorism: "Industrial development, rather than opening up society for the mass of the populace by expanding opportunities for employment, has instead only expanded access to goods from a traditional elite to a much broader stratum, but still a minority, of the population." James Petras, *Politics and Social Forces in Chilean Development* (Berkeley and Los Angeles: University of California Press, 1969), p. 19. The usual optimistic assumption is that, as in the "developed" countries, the new opportunities will spread in time to the entire population. A major object here is to cast serious doubt on this assumption.

9. Galbraith, *op. cit.,* p. 4.
10. Baran, *op. cit.,* p. 228.
11. J. K. Galbraith, for example, claims that in India the introduction of maize hybrids would be beneficial, but tractors would not. *Op. cit.,* p. 56. Numerous other examples of inappropriate technologies are cited in René Dumont, *False Start in Africa,* 2d ed., rev. (New York: Praeger, 1969), and Guy Hunter, *Modernizing Peasant Societies* (London: Oxford University Press, 1969).
12. This was clearly evident in four Turkish villages studied by Jan Hinderink and Mubeccel B. Kiray. See their *Social Stratification as an Obstacle to Development* (New York: Praeger, 1970). Similarly, increases in economic productivity as a whole may yield only entrepreneurial benefits. See Celso Furtado, *Development and Underdevelopment* (Berkeley and Los Angeles: University of California Press, 1967), pp. 5-6.
13. N. Eisenstadt, *The Political Systems of Empires* (Glencoe, Ill.: Free Press, 1963).
14. I am indebted to Professor N. J. Demerath for drawing my attention to this term, and to "instrumentalism," which approximates my concept of producerism. Both are propounded in his paper, "Rationalization and Instrumental Capacity," presented to the Midwest Sociological Society Meeting, April 17, 1970. My usage differs somewhat from his.
15. A. J. Jaffe, *People, Jobs and Economic Development* (New York: Free Press, 1959), p. 268.
16. Furtado, *op. cit.,* p. 170, is among several economists who have deplored "excess" production capacity in poor countries. In the works cited by Dumont and Hunter, numerous examples of this are given. Only half of the land that could be irrigated by projects in West Bengal and Bihar was actually irrigated, while multiple cropping made possible by irrigated lands was only sparsely practiced. See N. V. Sovani, "Non-economic Aspects of India's Economic Development," in Ralph J. Braibanti and J. J. Spengler (eds.), *Administration and Economic Development in India* (Durham, N.C.: Duke University Press, 1963), p. 261.
17. The best known is that proposed by Marx and countered by economist Walt W. Rostow, whose stage theory is outlined in his *The Stages of Economic Growth: A Non-Communist Manifesto* (New York: Cambridge University Press, 1960).
18. Baran, *op. cit.,* p. 21.
19. *Ibid.,* p. 51.
20. *Ibid.,* p. 177.
21. The central importance of the production-consumption mix, terms closely related to my usage here, has also been stressed by Furtado, *op. cit.,* p. 80.
22. This dualism has been noted by many economists including Furtado, *Ibid.,* pp. 129, 142.
23. J. M. Echavarria, "A Theoretical Model of Development Applicable to Latin America," in E. deVries and J. M. Echavarria (eds.), *Social Aspects of Economic Growth in Latin America* (Paris: UNESCO, 1963), p. 35.
24. H. A. Landsberger, "The Labor Elite: Is it Revolutionary?" in S. M. Lipset and A. Solari (eds.), *Elites in Latin America* (New York: Oxford University Press, 1967), p. 289.
25. I. L. Horowitz, *Three Worlds of Development* (New York: Oxford University Press, 1966), p. 396.
26. This highly descriptive term was coined by Frantz Fanon. For his fresh but somewhat distorted psychoanalytic views of the world's underlings, see his *The Wretched of the Earth* (New York: Grove Press, 1968) translated by Constance Farrington.

27. C. W. Mills, *Power, Politics and People* (New York: Ballantine, 1963), p. 152.
28. *Ibid.,* p. 153.
29. Echavarria, *loc. cit.,* p. 36.
30. H. A. Landsberger, in Lipset and Solari (eds.), *op. cit.,* pp. 256-300.
31. P. Mercier, "Problems of Social Stratification in West Africa (1954)," in I. Wallerstein (ed.), *Social Change: The Colonial Situation* (New York: Wiley, 1966), p. 343.
32. This is what Horowitz called the mental set of developing man. See Horowitz, *op. cit.,* p. 326.
33. Such work is often the result of a misplaced sentimentality and a yearning for an idealized rural life, but more serious analysis is possible. See, for example, Jacques Ellul, *The Technological Society,* trans. by J. Wilkinson (New York: Alfred A. Knopf, 1964).
34. Baran, *op. cit.,* p. 174.
35. Irma Adelman and Cynthia T. Morris, *Society, Politics and Economic Development* (Baltimore: Johns Hopkins Press, 1967), pp. 272-273.
36. E. J. Hobsbawm, *Industry and Empire* (New York: Pantheon, 1968), p. 75.
37. G. Germani, "Social Change and Intergroup Conflicts," in I. L. Horowitz (ed.), *The New Sociology* (New York: Oxford University Press, 1964), p. 398.
38. *Ibid.,* p. 402.
39. See H. B. Chenery and M. Bruno, "Development Alternatives in an Open Economy," *Economic Journal,* March, 1962, pp. 79-103. Cf. also Furtado, *op. cit.,* pp. 138-139, 170.
40. David Felix, "Latin America: Take-offs into Unsustained Growth," *Social Research,* August, 1969, calculated from ECLA expenditure estimates, U.N. Economic Commission for Latin America,*The Process of Industrial Development in Latin America* (New York: United Nations, 1966), pp. 242-243. I am grateful for access to a draft of this paper prior to its publication. It has greatly influenced my comments on import substitution that follow.
41. David Felix, "Monetarists, Structuralists, and Import-Substituting Industrialization: A Critical Appraisal," *Studies in Comparative International Development,* vol. 1, no. 10, 1965, p. 149.
42. See the articles by D. Felix already cited and his "The Dilemma of Import Substitution—Argentina," in G. F. Papanek (ed.), *Development Policy—Theory and Practice* (Cambridge, Mass.: Harvard University Press, 1968), pp. 51-91.
43. *Ibid.,* p. 56.
44. For example, assuming a capital/output ratio of 3, Rostow argues that about 10 per cent of the Net National Product is required for "take-off," while Ward calls for 12 to 15 per cent investment to generate a growth rate of 3 to 5 per cent. See W. W. Rostow, *op. cit.,* and B. Ward, *The Rich Nations and the Poor Nations* (New York: W. W. Norton, 1963). Both are arguing for increased producerism, but they ignore the dominant existence of consumerism. If, of course, the latter is eradicated, their models calling for asceticism and work become more relevant.
45. African elites that exhibit strong drives for personal rather than social wealth have been called "kleptocracies" by S. Andreski. See his *The African Predicament* (London: Joseph, 1968). For an equally distempered view of Latin America, see his *Parasitism and Subversion* (New York: Pantheon, 1967).
46. Baran doubts this. "The economic development in underdeveloped countries," he claims, "is profoundly inimical to the dominant interests in the advanced capitalist countries. Supplying many important raw materials to the industrialized countries, providing their corporations with vast profits and investment outlets, the backward world has always represented the indispensable hinterland of the highly developed capitalist West." Baran, *op. cit.,* pp. 11-12. Less willing to join the barricades and more trusting of humanitarian pronouncements of rich-country leaders, I am more optimistic that the developed countries can yet follow the requisites of their long-range interests. This perhaps may mean that corporations must be subordinated by national governments—by no means an easy task.
47. Western pressures are not always entirely to blame for high consumerism. The Vietnamese government, for example, continued to issue import licenses for luxury

consumer goods despite the urging of American advisors to use the commercial import program for more productive but less glamorous goods. See John D. Montgomery, "Political Dimensions of Foreign Aid," in Ralph J. Braibanti and J. J. Spengler (eds.), *Tradition, Values and Socio-economic Development* (Durham, N.C.: Duke University Press, 1961).

4.

communications
theory of
development

The availability of the mass media, or at least the potential for widespread use of them, is one of the major factors that makes development of today's poor countries radically different from that of the developed countries a century ago. As such, mass communications have been given wide attention in development literature. There are three competing general theories regarding the value of communications (of all types) for development. Attempts have also been made to distinguish between the effects of different media. Most of the remainder of theoretical writing on the subject seeks to elaborate on the real or ideal functions—especially learning—of modern mass media. These approaches are considered in this chapter, and their relevance to the consumerism theory of development is examined.[1] The resulting view of the media, that they are a developmental factor via their differential consumerism and producerism effects, is the framework used in Part II, the empirical case study of Latin American television.

GENERAL THEORIES

It is widely believed that increasing the mass media stimulates economic development. This is maintained by what has been called the "Communist theory of media use,"[2] which specifies that the media should be used as a key organizing device. Such *positive theories* have also been held by non-communist scholars and are the official position of the United Nations. Alternate theories view communications networks as merely a product of development, not a causal factor in growth. This may be called a *neutral theory.* It is held implicitly by developmentalists who exclude communications from their sets of relevant growth variables. Developing countries that once formally subscribed to simplistic positive theories have often modified their view to correspond to their unhappy experiences. They hold an implicit theory of "disillusionment,"[3] namely, that the media aid neither education nor planning but stimulate the masses to "unrealistic" material demands. This constitutes a *negative theory* of communications that is grounded in experience. But it reflects actual failure, rather than a categorical refutation, of the long-term potential of the media as a developmental weapon.

Daniel Lerner, a leading American scholar in this field, clearly subscribes to the positive type of theory. "The modernization process begins," he claims, "with new public communication . . . the diffusion of new ideas and new information which stimulate people to want to behave in new ways."[4] The new media are causal factors of growth and the process is irreversible:

> First, the direction of change is always from oral to media system (no known case exhibits change in the reverse direction). Second, the degree of change in communication behavior appears to correlate significantly with other behavioral changes in the social sytem.[5]

He ignores here the fact that the media impact is often from *outside* of the system or nation state. In his major work, Lerner concludes that by "empathy" with the media the audience is subject to "radical changes in self."[6] These changes toward modernity are not, however, naïvely assumed to be developmental. In his introduction to Lerner's book, David Riesman has concluded that "... the continuous turmoil that the new media can encourage, and the new consumer goods entice, would seem to be new."[7] Lerner has clearly recognized that an evolutionary framework is not entirely suitable to analyze the novel experience of underdeveloped countries. He has also documented the potentially explosive element of consumerism in the "modernization" transmitted by the media.

To Karl Deutsch, both exposure to mass media and exposure to a multidimensional "modernity" (exposure to rumors, demonstrations of machinery or merchandise) are elements of, and indicators for, social mobilization. The latter is apparently necessary for economic development, though not sufficient to ensure it:

> Sustained income growth is very unlikely without social mobiliza-
> tion, but a good deal of social mobilization may be going on even in
> the absence of per capita income growth such as occurs in countries
> with poor resources or investment policies, and with rapid popula-
> tion growth. In such cases, social mobilization still would generate
> pressures for an expansion of government services and hence of the
> government sector, even in a relatively stagnant or conceivably
> retrograde economy.[8]

Unfortunately for logical rigor, Deutsch included income growth as an indicator of social mobilization. He was primarily concerned with the effects of mobilization on political behavior. In the absence of economic growth social mobilization can lead to pressures on the government as indicated above. In a homogeneous society it normally promotes increased integration, while in a heterogeneous one it may exacerbate existing rifts. Nonetheless, with the exception of the conditions cited by·Deutsch above, the implicit theory is that exposure to the media and "modernity" (both elements of social mobilization) facilitate economic development. This assumption will not be made here because the content of the media and type of modernity (producerism or consumerism) diffused are considered to be crucially important.

Work done on behalf of the United Nations using cross-national data has confirmed that there is a strong correlation between media development and economic level, urbanization, industrialization, and literacy.[9] This is compatible with either neutral or positive theories.

The United Nations apparently adopts the latter, and therefore recommends the widespread expansion of the mass media irrespective of economic level. Thus they suggest minimum targets for all countries as follows: For each 100 persons there should be ten daily newspapers, five radio receivers, two cinema seats, and two television sets.[10] If these rates are accepted as a target to be achieved, the problem then becomes one of priorities and the uses of the media.

THE DIFFERENTIAL VALUE OF THE MEDIA

The United Nations recommendation to develop more or less simultaneously all of the modern media has not been unanimously accepted even in principle by policy makers and communications experts. The introduction and growth of television has been the most strongly resisted. Note, for example, the hostility expressed by a leading communications scholar:

> Television is expensive. The sets are expensive; production is expensive; transmission is expensive: It requires a great deal of electricity and employs vast amounts of talent in writing, in acting, in repair and maintenance. Whenever the government has kept television noncommercial, financing has been difficult, for the cost of keeping an adequate supply of interesting material in production to fill the air waves for many hours a day is horrendous.[11]

Undoubtedly the medium is expensive, but broadcasting many hours a day in the United States fashion is not, perhaps, an absolute imperative. Britain's much more limited daily schedule is an indication of this. Nor need the admittedly high costs be wasted if the developmental yield is maximized. Hiding costs in the private sector by permitting commercial utilization of television may help the public sector's budgetary accounting, but it does not necessarily help the economy as a whole, since the developmental usage of the media is usually neglected in the process. Private television is almost always devoted exclusively to entertainment and sales.

The most influential seer of media differences in contemporary society, even though he is often denied full recognition as a "serious" scholar, is undoubtedly H. Marshall McLuhan. He has invented his own terminology, methodology, and literary style to produce a new paradigm for understanding media which cannot, he claims, be judged in "literary" terms; that is, by what he calls "linear," continuous reasoning and logic.

The validity and usefulness of this "new" *weltanschauung* has been acclaimed by disparate enthusiasts. Radical youth may like it because it proclaims them to be qualitatively (psychically) different from their seniors, who continue to plod along with their linear, print-oriented thought patterns. Despite the fact that McLuhan's first book[12] was a scathing attack on them, advertising men find his later deemphasis of media content a perfect ideology to excuse their practices, even if it does not fully justify them. Outside a small band of ardent followers, McLuhan has been largely ignored by conventional scholars. As with Marx, McLuhan's following seems to respond to the seductive nature of a simple all-encompassing explanatory scheme. In this case, McLuhan has substituted media characteristics for the Marxian relations of production. With this scheme he can interpret history,[13] explain contemporary events, and predict the outlines of the future.[14]

As with Marx, however, it should not be necessary to adopt his whole system in order to find it useful. What McLuhan has to say on specific aspects of the media may still be worth examining individually. Thus his views on the importance of media content, differences between types of media, and the world context of communication are considered here.

McLuhan's thoughts on the content of media are stated strongly and succinctly as follows:

> Our conventional response to all media, namely that it is how they are used that counts, is the numb stance of the technological idiot. For the "content" of a medium is like the juicy piece of meat carried by the burglar to distract the watchdog of the mind. . . . The effect of the movie form is not related to its program content.[15]

Boulding has formalized this in his statement that "a social system is largely structured by the nature of the media in which communications are made, not by the content of these communications."[16] Now it is true that there are what might be called "first order" consequences of changing from one media to another. The printing press and television network undoubtedly have an impact that transcends their content, and this is the impact that McLuhan emphasizes to the exclusion of "lesser" media effects.

Such a "grand theoretical" view, however, overlooks many important details, even if these are not of world historical significance. Nazi Germany, for example, was not particularly unique in its media structure, for several other nations possessed close approximations to its print-radio media mix. But surely the differences in media *content* made Germany sufficiently different from Britain, the United States, and France to make it a qualitatively unique environment. If, for example, Jews had been able to determine the *content* of the Nazi media, is it not possible that the outcome for them might have been different? Can we completely discount the numerous studies of media content and claim that whether gangster films or ballet, exhortations to consume or do-it-yourself, programs shown on television have *no* differential effects on the audience? Clearly the advertising followers of McLuhan think otherwise—that content counts—and the seller of merchandise backs this conviction with money.

McLuhan does have one useful statement on content. He claims epigrammatically that "it's misleading to suppose there's any basic difference between education and entertainment."[17] This could be interpreted as meaning "anything goes," or "the medium is the message," but in context the statement was directed at the educational purist. His point was that people are educated by their entertainment, the things that they enjoy. But this, apparently, should accentuate the importance of content; by this interpretation even banal and trivial "entertainment" is insistently educating the public. The educationally conceived pills should therefore be sweetened to compete.

Conventional students of communication stress the content of the media (this approach is followed by looking for consumerism and producerism in the media), while McLuhan stresses differences between them. His major dichotomy is between "hot" and "cool" media. The former do not require much participation by the recipient, but the latter do. The designation of a medium is crucial since McLuhan claims that its effect ". . . on the structure of society depends very much on its temperature."[18] Boulding has conceded that there are qualitative differences between face-to-face communication, print, radio, and television. But he doubts that simplistically labelling the latter "cool," while designating print as "hot," in the McLuhan fashion can serve much purpose. It does of course suggest easily distinct historical epochs and thus fits nicely into McLuhan's system. Since both speech (primitive communication) and television are classified as "cool," the McLuhan cycle is closed—in his words we are returning to the "tribal village."

The gross distinctions between media are doubtless necessary for the establishment of the media superstructure in McLuhan's system. In the analysis that follows, the differences are taken to be less marked, although emphasis will be on the most recently developed, television. The advent of this medium is not assumed, as McLuhan would reason, to usher in a new era or developmental stage.

The modern world is dealt with ambiguously because of the classification scheme devised by McLuhan. He recognizes that the contemporary media network is entirely new, but he then develops this insight as the part metaphorical, part serious, idea of a return to primitivism. One of McLuhan's admirers comments on this in the following way:

> A whole generation in America has grown up in the T.V. environment, and already these millions of people, twenty-five and under, have the same kind of sensory reactions as African tribesmen. The same thing is happening all over the world. The world is growing into a huge tribe, a ... *global village,* in a *seamless web* of electronics.[19]

Or as the master himself has said, "we live in a single constricted space resonant with tribal drums."[20] Very heady stuff indeed! But what does it all mean?

The TV generation, we are told, are like preliterates, but the analogy cannot reasonably be pushed too far (McLuhan of course doesn't spell out his arguments in linear or logical form). True, today's youth rely more on sound and sight for their communication than did the preceding "print" generation, and in this sense they may more closely resemble the primitives. But not only can they converse (the primitives' only mode), read print, and hear radio (as did their parents), they also participate in the highly technical and decidedly non-primitive communication (one-way) medium, television.

And what is the global village into which we will be (or have been—McLuhan is unclear on this point) retribalized? Clearly it cannot be a return to a social life dominated by face-to-face oral patterns of communication. It represents, at best, the notion of an international audience made possible by electronic communications, to which the world's real tribesmen can "plug in" without going through the stage of literacy. The unifying factor may be the modern media, but the messages they carry are not in fact universal. Thus there are quarrels in our "village" that cannot be automatically settled simply by expanding communication networks.

That McLuhan's grasp of the international setting is rudimentary may be illustrated by the following passage in which he maintains his position that the media have effects *sui generis*. Here though, he is apparently less sure of the desirability of the "global village," indeed he would rather postpone its development:

> If TV was simply eliminated from the United States scene, it would be a very good thing. Just as radio has a most malignant effect in Africa or [sic] Algeria, or China—in highly auditory cultures, radio drives these people nearly mad with paranoia and tribal intensity— TV, in a highly visual culture, drives us inward in depth into a totally non-visual universe of involvement. It is destroying our entire fabric of society in a short time. If you understand its dynamics, you would choose to eliminate it as soon as possible. TV changes the sensory and psychic life. It is an oriental form of experience, giving people a somber, profound sense of involvement.[21]

The new experience is not literally "oriental" as McLuhan claims, but entirely novel. There are indeed worldwide communications systems (although they are not "seamless webs" as Wolfe claimed) that can, by their structure and content, have very real consequences for the economic development of countries. But the effects of these media systems are viewed here to be in part a product of their content, not merely their form as McLuhan implies. As such, they are like the other "determinants" of economic development.

THE MEDIA AS MANIPULATIVE OR LIBERATING DEVICES

Since the media are invariably controlled by a small group of people, be they government personnel or private operators, they always have a manipulating potential. Indeed, by the necessary selection of information to be transmitted, no matter how carefully this selection is made, there is always a slant given to the reportage of human events. So the problem of manipulation is a matter of degree. The United Nations General Assembly no doubt recognizes this, but proclaims that "freedom of information is one of the basic freedoms and that it is essential to the furtherance and protection of all other freedoms."[22] The media, they claim, should be tools for freely disseminating information, and to fulfill this liberating task there should be "a diversity of sources of news and opinion."[23] Unfortunately this appears to be impractical in developed and underdeveloped countries alike.

Schramm argues that the media should not be used just for the transmission of orders from a ruling elite to their charges, but as a communications channel whereby the masses can participate in national government and development planning.[24] This is a rather utopian exhortation. It is difficult to institute appropriate feedback systems in the modern media. The rulers and media controllers are seldom actively interested in fostering perfect democracy—they have too much to lose. And finally, the media are *not* distributed evenly throughout the population.[25] But despite the impracticality of Schramm's recommendation, it cannot be denied that the (unutilized) potential for such use of the media remains. The same is generally true of the more detailed functions that the media are claimed to serve, and which will now be briefly examined.

THE FUNCTIONS OF THE MEDIA

Communications, claims Schramm, must be used to induce greater effort on all social, political, and economic fronts.[26] The essential functions, he continues, are as follows:[27] to contribute to the feeling of nation-ness, and permit participation in national planning—this has already been described as rather "utopian." The media should provide the people with role-models of their new parts (if, of course, they ever get the chance to play new parts), and should "prepare the people to play their role as a nation among nations" (the meaning of this function varies with one's interpretation of "normal" international relations). Finally, the media should help teach necessary skills—by which he means more advanced ones than currently existing—and extend the effective market, that is, stimulate demand. My attention will be primarily on these last two functions.

Schramm[28] and the economist Harry T. Oshima[29] have both emphasized the multiplicative effects of mass communication. Oshima opposes the "balanced" growth thesis of economic development proposed by Ragnar Nurkse and the "unbalanced" proposals of Hirschman and Domar. Instead, he calls for a "selective" approach which would give developmental emphasis to a part of every economic sector following a kind of stratified sample. Successes would then be disseminated throughout the sector by the mass communications media. This could clearly be useful for organizational innovations, but it would do little more than provoke envy where the demonstrated innovation required capital investment. For example, it would seem useless (or worse) to demonstrate the benefits of tractor plowing to a poor farmer who can barely feed his draught animals.

It is clear that all of these functions are ideal. In practice the media have often served as the entertainment part of the classic "bread and circuses" control mechanism, a sop to forestall demands for structural reforms and maintain the position of the dominant elites. Indeed, democratically elected governments have been overthrown in part by the influence of an "unfavorable" press controlled by powerful minority interests. The media have been used to stimulate hate for external enemies and politically weak internal minorities, a fact which gives modern wars and witch hunts a unique hysteria and pervasiveness. Alternatively, where the media are not controlled by a central authority, they may stimulate disunity where coexistence, which is usually the product of relative isolation, had hitherto existed. The actual functions of the media, then, are by no means entirely benign and "progressive."

The Media and Learning. There seems to be little doubt that people learn from media participation, as indeed they do from all existential experiences. This is perhaps the most immediate function of the media. Much of this learning is "unconscious." For example, one communications expert remarks as follows:

> Parents note, not always approvingly, how children learn "singing commercials," slogans, vocabulary and customs from television, without trying to, without even realizing they are learning. In other words, all our experience with the mass media illustrates how easy it is, voluntarily or involuntarily, to learn from them.[30]

The problem at issue here is to determine what kinds of learning contribute the most to economic development. It is generally agreed that it is necessary to teach the audience the market facilities available to them. This in turn stimulates market activity and promotes individual motivation by offering material incentive. This teaching is apparently easily transmitted. Secondly, the media can teach productive skills and complement formal education. This can be particularly useful where educational resources are scarce and unevenly distributed.[31]

Formal teaching and skill training through the media are not as simple as market stimulation, in part because the former is not widely practiced by the developed countries. From Western research findings, however, it is apparent that a two-way communication system reinforces this type of learning.[32] Such findings have been widely applicable, and "feedback" programs have been employed with relative success in India, Jordan (radio forums), China, and the Philippines.[33] For efficient feedback it has been necessary to make programming as local as possible.[34] But this has the disadvantage of higher costs than "mass" programming, and, by reinforcing localism, it may tend to negate nation-building efforts.

PRODUCERISM, CONSUMERISM, AND MASS MEDIA POTENTIALS

The underdeveloped countries have the advantage of being able to utilize the modern media in their development efforts. Such media were not available to developed countries at the "same" economic stage. Developmental uses must, however, be invented by them, since the media have seldom been consciously used to this end, at least in the West. Successful educational programs, if they teach usable skills to the mass population, would clearly constitute elements of what has been called "producerism." Put to such use, the media have great developmental potential.

Clearly, too, the media can usefully stimulate the market and aspirations. One "expert" finds this sufficient reason to permit commercial underwriting and control of the mass media. He sees advertising as a "powerful instrument of development," because "it is a way of facilitating the distribution of commodities, broadening the market, and making people aware of possibilities with which they would not otherwise be familiar."[35] But commercial control may preclude or greatly limit the educational or "producerism" uses of the media, and stimulate only the "modern" sector of the market. As Schramm,[36] Lerner,[37] and others have warned, there must be a correspondence between what the masses are induced to *want*, and what they can conceivably *get*. If the goods advertised are predominantly those in the cosmopolitan sector, "glamorous" imports or import substitutes, the disadvantages of excess consumerism will be in effect. The simplistic assumption that any media development is *ipso facto* beneficial must therefore be abandoned, even, as Lerner notes, in United States government programs overseas.[38]

The developmental impact of the media can therefore be maximized by their use as teaching devices and multipliers, and by the propagation of an ideology in line with the developmental attitudes set (highly work-oriented, negative to the imported Western "ideologies" of advertising). This may, of course, include the stimulation of realistic mass markets. Even if we concede the "end of ideology" in the West, we should recognize that in the Third World it has scarcely begun. By packaging the developmental ideology in nationalistic rhetoric, it may be made more effective as it has been to a degree in Japan and China. To be believed, the ideological exhortations must be accompanied by structural changes including some distribution of the benefits accruing to past sacrifice.[39] Nationalism permits appeals to "sacrifice for your country" and can help to redefine modernism—what is desirable and fashionable—in terms suitable to the nation's level of wealth. This redefinition is difficult in a world of international communications. For example, a sophisticated public transport network in an urban center may be more efficient and less of a drain on developmental resources than a private automobile and road system. But the latter is often tenaciously regarded as more "modern" and "cosmopolitan," and hence more desirable.

NOTES

1. For a brief summary of the argument offered here, see Alan Wells, "Communication and Development: The Relevance of Media Content," *The Sociological Quarterly*, 12, Winter 1971, pp. 95-99.

2. Ithiel De Sola Pool, "Mass Media and Politics in the Modernization Process," in Lucian B. Pye (ed.), *Communications and Political Development* (Princeton: Princeton University Press, 1963), p. 241.
3. *Ibid.*, pp. 236-238.
4. Daniel Lerner, "Toward a Communication Theory of Modernization," in Pye (ed.), *op. cit.*, p. 348.
5. Daniel Lerner, "Communication Systems and Social Systems," in Wilbur Schramm (ed.), *Mass Communications* (Urbana: University of Illinois Press, 1960), p. 133. The correlations referred to here will be examined further in Chapter 8.
6. Daniel Lerner, *The Passing of Traditional Society* (New York: Free Press, 1968), especially chap. 11.
7. *Ibid.*, p. 5.
8. Karl W. Deutsch, "Social Mobilization and Political Development," in J. L. Finkle and R. W. Gable (eds.), *Political Development and Social Change* (New York: Wiley, 1966), p. 213.
9. UNESCO, *Mass Media in the Developing Countries* (Paris: UNESCO, 1961), p. 17.
10. *Ibid.*, p. 16.
11. Ithiel de Sola Pool, "Communications and Development," in M. Weiner (ed.), *Modernization: The Dynamics of Growth* (New York: Basic Books, 1966), p. 108.
12. H. Marshall McLuhan, *The Mechanical Bride: Folklore of Industrial Man* (New York: The Vanguard Press, 1951).
13. H. M. McLuhan, *The Gutenberg Galaxy: The Making of Topographic Man* (Toronto: University of Toronto Press, 1962).
14. Present and future are the subjects of his *Understanding Media: The Extension of Man* (New York: McGraw-Hill, 1964), and (with Quentin Fiore) *The Medium is the Message* (New York: Random House, 1967).
15. *Understanding Media,* quoted by H. Rosenberg, in G. E. Stearn (ed.), *McLuhan: Hot and Cool* (New York: Dial Press, 1967), p. 198.
16. K. Boulding in Stearn (ed.), *op. cit.*, p. 59.
17. *Ibid.*, p. 116.
18. Boulding, *loc. cit.*, p. 60.
19. Tom Wolfe, "suppose he is what he sounds like, the most important thinker since newton, darwin, freud, einstein, and pavlov [sic] —what if he is right?" (Article title appears in lowercase. The subject pronoun refers to McLuhan.) In Stearn (ed.), *op. cit.*, p. 19.
20. T. Wolfe quoting McLuhan, *loc. cit.*, p. 18.
21. H. Marshall McLuhan, in an interview with Stearn, *op. cit.*, p. 301.
22. General Assembly, Resolution 313 (IV), quoted in UNESCO, *op. cit.*, p. 15.
23. U.N. Conference on Freedom of Information, Final Act, Resolution 1, quoted in *Ibid.*, p. 15.
24. Wilbur Schramm, *Mass Media and National Development* (Stanford, Calif.: Stanford University Press, 1964), pp. 37-38.
25. S. C. Dube has illustrated the sectoral disparities, especially of "luxury" television. The less developed sectors (he generalizes from the Indian situation) still have competing and autonomous traditional networks. See his "A Note on Communication in Economic Development," in Lerner and Schramm, *op. cit.*, p. 95.
26. They may also have a very useful "play" function. For an exposition of this argument, see William Stephenson, *The Play Theory of Mass Communication* (Chicago: University of Chicago Press, 1967), especially pp. 95-99.
27. Wilbur Schramm, "Communication Development and the Development Process," in Pye (ed.), *op. cit.*, pp. 38ff.
28. Wilbur Schramm, "Communication and Change," in Lerner and Schramm (eds.), *op. cit.*, p. 17.
29. See his article "The Strategy of Selective Growth and the Role of Communications," in *Ibid.*, pp. 76-91.
30. Wilbur Schramm, *Mass Media and National Development* (Stanford, Calif.: Stanford University Press, 1964), p. 127.

31. H. Dienzeide, *European Broadcasting Union Review,* 75B (1962), pp. 45-58, quoted in *Ibid.,* pp. 165-166.
32. For example, see the findings of Elihu Katz and Paul Lazarsfeld, *Personal Influence* (Glencoe, Ill.: Free Press, 1955), and the work of K. Hovland and associates in the Yale Communications Program.
33. See the chapters on these countries in Lerner and Schramm (eds.), *op. cit.*
34. Schramm, *op. cit.,* p. 123.
35. Ithiel de Sola Pool, "Communications and Development," in Weiner (ed.), *op. cit.,* p. 108.
36. Schramm, *op. cit.,* p. 131.
37. D. Lerner, "International Cooperation and Communication in National Development," in Lerner and Schramm, *op. cit.,* pp. 104-105—where there is no correspondence between desires and their attainment, he refers to a "revolution of rising frustrations."
38. *Ibid.,* p. 105.
39. Schramm has said that the media should exhort the masses to "tighten their belts, harden their muscles, work longer, and wait for rewards." See his "Communication and Change" in D. Lerner and N. Schramm (eds.) *op. cit.,* pp 18-19. But this is of no avail if a conspicuous upper class fails to set an ascetic example.

Part II

The New Media and Development: A Case Study of Television in Latin America

5.

latin america and the world distribution of the mass media

In Chapter 4, it was argued that the mass media are potentially powerful tools for achieving rapid economic growth. They are based on modern technological devices that were not available in the early phases of the rich countries' growth. Wise usage can therefore greatly help the poor countries in their attempts to catch the more affluent. The media, especially radio and television which don't require literacy, can play a major role in mass mobilization and social change. But they can also be mere symbols of modernity, or worse, carriers of parasitic consumerism. That is, they may encourage the affluent segment of the population to participate in the material consumer culture of countries having a much stronger economic base.

The availability of the media in Latin America relative to the other world regions, and then the distribution of the modern media (especially television) and its relationship to economic levels in the Latin American countries, are the subjects of this chapter. It will be shown that given their low levels of economic development the distribution of the mass media is relatively advanced in these countries. After this quantitative base of media availability has been established, the remaining chapters are devoted to the uses of the last to be introduced in the region, television.

THE WORLD DISTRIBUTION OF MEDIA

The spread of mass media throughout the globe generally follows the distribution of wealth. Countries with high per capita Gross National Products tend to have high per capita media consumption, but GNP per capita are indicators of wealth and only a guide to contemporary differences. Other variables such as literacy, urbanization, and features of the countries' occupational structure are also related to media use (see Table III); indeed, urbanization is a better predictor of cinema seating capacity, and the percentage employed in non-agricultural employment of television availability, than is per capita income. Even if multiple correlations were used, it is doubtful that prediction of media use in any particular country could be made in anything but a statistical sense; that is, we cannot accurately predict that rises in, for example, literacy or GNP will lead to specified increases in media consumption in the future. Too many personal decisions (for example, permission to engage in broadcasting operation) and international influences (whether or not communications equipment, including newsprint, is made available) preclude accurate prediction from purely national gross economic data. Thus, although the zero order correlations between the indices shown in Table III are quite high, their policy implications—whether or not to expand the media to assist growth—are by no means self-evident.

In many countries the growth of the media, especially the new electronic ones, has been proportionately much more rapid than concurrent changes in the more static social variables commonly taken to be valuable predictors. After a sophisticated cross-national correlation analysis two researchers conclude that:

> urbanization seems, on the basis of 1961 data, no longer to be so basic to the growth of literacy and the mass media as Lerner had found it to be on the basis of data approximately ten years

older. . . . There is serious doubt that any single pattern will explain
the differences that appear to exist by regions and cultures.[1]

They exclude international influences—political pressures, trade, aid,
and investment arrangements—which might help explain these
differences. These variables, of course, would present a formidable
measurement problem that would have to be overcome before they
could be included in such quantitative regression analyses.

The underdeveloped countries usually have higher media rates
than the developed countries had when they were at similar "stages"
of economic development. The most recent media, radio and
television, of course, have spread to countries that are economically
several decades "behind" the levels enjoyed in the West at the time
the media were invented. Indeed, as has been noted, the United
Nations has set minimum standards for the distribution of these
media that it recommends, irrespective of economic wealth.

The United Nations standard rates have not been universally
achieved in low income regions as Table IV illustrates. Asia, the
Middle East, and Africa—in spite of the inclusion of South
Africa—were far from the standards in the early sixties. Latin
America, however, exceeded the standards for radio receivers and
cinema seats while falling only a little short of the target for
newspaper circulation. For all three media the region has much
higher rates than the other underdeveloped regions. The latter have
similar low rates for newspapers and cinema seats, while South East
Asia exhibits a unique paucity of radio receivers.

Within each region there are variations from one country to the
next that cannot be accounted for by economic factors alone. This
may be illustrated by data for the eight South Asian countries
presented in Table V. Similar variations can be expected in the other
regions. It should be noted that these countries, especially the three
richest, Malaya, the Philippines, and Ceylon, are much closer to
achieving the U.N. standards for radio than for newspapers. By 1967,
thanks perhaps to the American presence and transistors, Thailand
actually exceeded the target figure. In addition, the expansion of the
electronic media has generally tended to be much more rapid during
the period covered by Table V than has newspaper growth[2] (note
columns 2, 3, and 4; and 5, 6, and 7 in Table V). Thailand is
conspicuous in the development of both radio and television given its

extremely low level of wealth. Dizard[3] estimated in the early sixties that on a "typical" day in Bangkok "almost half" of the city's population of 1.8 million citizens watches television. Once television is introduced, it is invariably the fastest expanding medium. Since it also has potentially the greatest effect on its audience, it will now be considered in more detail.

Television has expanded very rapidly since the mid-fifties in all major areas of the globe. Table VI shows the expansion of sets in use in the underdeveloped regions. The most affluent areas—North America, Western and Eastern Europe—still have by far the highest saturation of the medium, but the rapid growth in all regions, including Latin America, is clearly ahead of economic growth rates and the economic levels that would seem necessary for the most expensive mass medium. Television is clearly one of the technological inputs that differentiates the poor countries of today from those of previous eras.

Although there are undoubtedly affluent individuals in poor countries, they alone are not sufficient to account for the television boom. Nor can a rich-sector explanation be held contrary to the phenomenon of poor-owned television receivers so often observed and remarked upon by travelling Westerners. The consumer potential of television sets is much higher than experiences in the West would indicate. A Japanese survey taken in 1959, for example, "indicated that almost 70% of that country's television set owners earned less than five hundred dollars."[4] Once television broadcasting is in operation, a TV set apparently acquires a very high consumer priority. The implications of this attractive and perhaps premature new medium in Latin America are the subject of following chapters.

MASS MEDIA AND ECONOMY IN LATIN AMERICA

It has been shown that when compared with the other underdeveloped regions, Latin America is well endowed with modern communications media (see Tables IV and VI), and even in 1960 exceeded the United Nations minimum standard for radio sets and cinema seats. The distribution for the region as a whole, however, is greatly inflated by the "Europeanized" countries in the extreme south, Argentina, Uruguay, and Chile. There are wide intercountry differences. As in Asia, the richest countries (as indicated by GNP per capita) have not necessarily been those with the highest levels of media development, as Table VII illustrates.

Although in general the top half of the countries in terms of per capita GNP are better endowed with media than the poorer half, there are notable discrepancies. Venezuela, for example, has a relatively low newspaper consumption, a fact that may in part be explained by its low literacy rate relative to its per capita GNP. By 1967 its newspaper consumption had actually declined to 62 per 1000 people.[5] Because the economy is based on the capital (rather than labor) intensive oil industry, the benefits of its indisputably high economic level are apparently not as widespread as in the more diversified economies of Argentina and Uruguay. Uruguay is easily ahead of all other countries in newspaper circulation, indeed on this indicator of development it is slightly ahead of the United States. Several of the countries approach, and in some cases greatly exceed, the cinema seating capacity of developed countries. (The source of Column 4, Table VII, credits the United Kingdom with 34, the United States with 32 cinema seats per 1000 population[6]). Relative to their economic levels, El Salvador and Peru have more than the expected number of radio sets, while Mexico[7], Costa Rica, and the Dominican Republic have too few. Clearly other factors in addition to GNP per capita determine a country's media consumption. These may include income distribution, the influence of internal political decisions, and external pressures and emulation.

Rank order correlations (Spearman's Rho) between the media indices presented in Table VII and the television receivers per 1000 population listed in Table IX confirm that the relations between the media and GNP are relatively strong (see Table VIII). Although the data do not warrant absolute confidence, some tentative inferences can be made. As would be expected, literacy is highly predictive of newspaper circulation, but its relationship to the electronic media is less strong. Indeed, literacy is the weakest predictor for these media. Radio and television availability, perhaps due to the high cost differential between them, are not highly correlated (rho = .79). Thus GNP per capita is the best predictor for the high cost medium, television, but not for radio, which is related a little more strongly to newspaper circulation.

Table IX shows the spread of television in Latin America by country. As already noted, the relationship between the availability of television sets and GNP per capita is high (rho = .89), but of course this is not perfect correlation. Thus, relative to their per capita GNP's, Argentina, Brazil, and Peru are disproportionately high on receiver density. This is in part due to differences in the number of years of broadcast programming in the countries of the region. Argentina, Brazil, Venezuela, and Mexico, for example, began television operations in the early 1950's,[8] several years before the rest of the continent. Thus with the exception of Mexico, no new stations were opened between 1964 and 1967 (see Table IX, Columns 2 and 3) in these countries. In the same period, Chile, which was a relative latecomer to television, experienced a transmitter boom, which no doubt stimulated the massive increase in receivers (Columns 4 and 5). Most of the other countries also showed considerable set increases between 1964 and 1967, even if these were less spectacular than Chile's. This is in marked contrast with the region's experience with radio receiver expansion during this period (see reference 8).

When compared to "developed countries," Latin America as a whole is seen to have a premature development of television relative to its economic development (see Diagram 5). For example, if Argentina followed the "highest" possible regression line for the Organization for Economic Cooperation and Development (OECD) countries, it would have only 50 television sets per 1000 people, not its present 141. Its current distribution of the medium exceeds that of Greece and Ireland, both of which have greater per capita GNP's. This may in part be explained by Argentina's early entry into TV broadcasting (1950) at least when compared to Greece, which started operations in the sixties. However, it also has more sets per capita than Austria or Denmark where broadcasting is well established and whose per capita GNP's are respectively more than double and nearly triple the Argentine figure.

The effects of late entry into television broadcasting, if anything, detract from the divergence illustrated in Diagram 5. Most of the OECD countries began broadcasting in the early fifties; that is, several years before the Latin American countries taken collectively entered the field. Only Argentina, Brazil, Mexico, and Venezuela started at a comparable time. According to U.N. statistics,[9] these countries had an estimated 20, 70, 90, and 20 thousand television sets, respectively, in use by 1954. The remaining countries reached the 10,000 receiver mark in the years indicated: Colombia, 1955; Guatemala, 1957; Dominican Republic, El Salvador, Uruguay, 1958; Peru, 1959; Panama, 1960; Costa Rica, 1962; Nicaragua and Chile, 1963; Ecuador, 1965; and Honduras and Haiti in 1966. Due to late entry, then, the Latin American curve should be *below* and to the right of the OECD regression, the reverse of the actual case.

The lag between the total set counts in Western Europe and Latin America is illustrated in Diagram 6. Since 1958, the available receivers in Western Europe have grown by a fairly constant 5 million sets per year. In Latin America the absolute growth has been lower, but the expansion between 1965 and 1967 compares favorably with that in Europe between 1956-1958, even though Europe was even then clearly more affluent than Latin America today. The rapid expansion of the media therefore is in this sense premature.

The relatively high media distribution in Latin America could be taken as a reflection of the sectoral growth of the region and its premature enjoyment of modern consumer gadgetry. Television ownership is apparently related to a different set of consumer priorities in the region than in the more affluent countries, especially since receivers in Latin America are generally imported and are usually about twice as expensive—after duties and tax have been added—as sets in the developed countries. Television ownership in the region is therefore considered to be a strong expression of modernity in itself. In addition, the set is one of the foremost channels for further inducing modern consumer tastes.

It has been established that television in Latin America has expanded relative to economic level more rapidly than would be expected from the experiences of more developed countries. The growth of the medium, as indicated by receivers in use, is similarly not directly dependent on economic growth, as shown in Table X. This table divides the sample of countries into three groups on the basis of their date of entry into television broadcasting. Countries in each group are arranged by their economic level (per capita GNP) in 1967.

Group I countries all reported television operations in 1955. With the exception of Argentina, receiver growth was much higher during the first five-year period than in the second, although clearly none of the countries approached a saturation point in 1965. For the first period, receiver expansion and short-term economic growth were closely related. With the exception of Colombia, which had the highest media but lowest economic growth rate, the ranks on each dimension were identical for each country. For the second period, however, the relationship breaks down. Television growth in Mexico, the fastest growing economy, was lower than in the Dominican Republic, which had experienced economic decline.

Group II countries had established television broadcasting operations after 1955 but before 1960. The growth of the media in Uruguay, Panama, and Peru compares favorably with Group I countries in their initial stage, indicating perhaps an expanded potential for media development now that its viability has been proven by the region's "lead" countries. New ventures are also more viable because they can now be integrated into international networks in the region. (Descriptions of the ABC networks are given in Chapter 6, which follows.) Media expansion for this group appears to be unrelated to economic growth: Uruguay's increase in receivers is due more to its late entry into TV broadcasting and its relatively high economic level, than to its performance in economic growth (which was negative for this period); while Nicaragua had the fastest economic expansion of this group of countries, but the slowest growth of the medium.

Group III countries began broadcasting during or after 1960. The very high rates of expansion for the four-year period exhibited by Chile, Costa Rica, and Ecuador again reflect late entry and compare well with the Group I countries in the early period. The Chilean expansion is also in part the result of its relatively high economic level. Again, the economic growth rates for the countries do not appear to be crucial to their media development. The spread of the medium must therefore be due to other factors. Foreign corporate and domestic government support for the television industry and high consumer demand are no doubt relevant here.

The raw data presented in this chapter only roughly indicate actual media use. In the Latin American countries television is clearly most accessible to the residents of the major urban centers. A group of communications researchers, for example, have noted that the overall low level of media development in Latin America vis-à-vis the United States is not noticeable in such centers: "Indeed," they add, "quite the opposite impression is created by the multiplicity of newsstands and book stores,"[10] and there is a wider choice of newspapers than in the North American city.

The more affluent city dweller is therefore by no means media starved. The professionals and technicians in the fourteen countries of the region that were studied by Deutschman and his associates read newspapers and magazines, and listened to radio just as frequently as their professional counterparts in the Midwest region of the United States. They read considerably more books, but watched fewer television programs—due probably to the infancy of the medium at the time of the study in the late 1950's—than the North Americans.[11] The Latin Americans were in more contact with all media (except for television in which they lagged slightly) than North Americans reporting in cross-cultural samples in four Midwest cities and in a United States national sample.[12] The Latin American professionals and technicians who had received training in the United States (at Michigan State University) as "change agents" did not use the media significantly more than a matched sample of Latin American counterparts with no United States experience. But they did listen to more United States programming in the region—perhaps because of their enhanced mastery of the language—and they paid less attention to communist (including Cuban) programs.[13] Thus the change agent program was evidently successful in fostering pro-United States sentiment, even if its overall media participation effectiveness remains in doubt: The program's effect was evidently ideological rather than developmental.

Media participation is not necessarily limited entirely to the urban upper and middle classes in the less developed countries. Even the most expensive medium, television, is not limited to this audience. The habit of communal watching in private homes and public facilities, as was the case in the early days of the medium in the United States and Europe, permits an audience of much greater size than the raw number of receivers would indicate.[14] Television viewing is still, however, undeniably concentrated in the urban areas, even if it is not restricted to their "modern" sectors. In conclusion, given the high availability of the medium (limited by economic levels, to be sure, but not by growth rates), the development problem is not one of whether or not to expand the medium, but of how the medium can be used to sustain real growth. Television was given special attention here because its impact, especially on illiterate or semi-literate audiences, is potentially great, and because of all the media it is the most obviously modern and the one in which international influences are maximized. The other media, of course, may mitigate its effects: We are dealing here with only one part of the mass communications network, which even as a whole is not the sole influence on the work and consumer patterns that help shape economic development.

NOTES

1. Wilbur Schramm and W. Lee Ruggels, "How Mass Media Systems Grow," in D. Lerner and W. Schramm (eds.), *Communications and Change in the Developing Countries* (Honolulu: East-West Center Press, 1967), p. 58.
2. Based on 1950-1962 growth rates and projected from 1962 media levels, the poorest regions should attain U.N. standards in the following years:

	Africa	Asia
Newspapers (10 per 100 persons)	2035	1992
Radios (5 per 100)	1968	1970
Cinema seats (2 per 100)	2042	1981

In both regions radio standards are expected to be achieved first.

Source: W. Schramm, *Mass Media and National Development* (Stanford, Calif.: Stanford University Press, 1964), p. 113.

3. W. Dizard, *Television: A World View* (Syracuse: Syracuse University Press, 1966), p. 47.
4. *Ibid.*, p. 46.
5. As reported in *U.N. Statistical Yearbook, 1969*, pp. 748-749, for the period 1965-1967. Declines were also registered by Argentina, Costa Rica, Dominican Republic, Honduras, and Ecuador. The remaining countries experienced no change or marginal increases in circulation.
6. More recent figures listed in *Ibid.*, pp. 552-555, show Argentina's rate to be a little above these developed countries. Countries reporting seating capacities for 1966-1968 generally suffered small declines in the rate reported in Table VII. Panama, however, lost half its capacity during the early sixties.
7. Rates calculated from radio receiver figures (*Ibid.*, p. 756) and mid-year population (*Ibid.*, pp. 56-57), both for 1968, indicate that Mexico greatly improved its position in the sixties—to 23 sets per 100 population. Other rapid growers were Argentina to 37 and impoverished Ecuador and Haiti to 14 and 1.7 sets per 100, respectively. Venezuela (17), Columbia (11), Nicaragua (5.7), Dominican Republic (3.8), El Salvador (12), and Honduras (5.8), all experienced *declines* in radio accessibility during this period.
8. J. Frappier, "U.S. Media Empire/Latin America," *NACLA Newsletter* (New York: North American Congress on Latin America), vol. 11, no. 9 (Jan., 1969), p. 1.
9. The receiver information that follows is from the *U.N. Statistical Yearbook*, various editions from 1956 to 1968.
10. P. J. Deutschman et al., *Communications and Social Change in Latin America* (New York: Praeger, 1968), p. 49.
11. *Ibid.*, Table VII, p. 53.
12. *Ibid.*, p. 62.
13. *Ibid.*, p. 62.
14. Communal viewing in the region was noted in *Ibid.*, p. 50.

6.

institutional transfer: the structure of united states interests in latin american television

It was stressed earlier that economic development within the confines of a state is never completely autonomous. It is always influenced from outside either by emulation of the more developed countries and target setting based on this, or by direct intervention in the economy by foreign governments and enterprises. The development of mass media is no exception. Most countries actively strive to improve their communications systems, or at least believe they should do so. For it is widely believed that such changes will stimulate economic growth generally, even though it is not known how the media do this. Television and radio both demand advanced technologies and high initial capital investment. In consequence, it is not surprising that developed countries, who have the necessary expertise and financial capability, are active in the spread of these mass media to less developed countries. The United States has provided the bulk of such assistance in recent years, although Britain, Germany, France, and Japan—the former colonial powers—are attempting to become increasingly active in the international media enterprise.

The dominance of North American over other foreign influences in the developing countries is most apparent in the case of television, particularly in Latin America, the internationally recognized sphere of influence for the United States. This United States dominance is due, in part, to its own advanced development of the medium: The bonanza domestic market in the United States showed signs of running out at a time when European expansion of television at home was still in a dynamic phase of its growth. The unique character of the United States home operations, especially its dominant commercial character, is therefore of great importance to the overseas development of the medium. (The character of United States television is outlined in Chapter 7, which follows.)

United States involvement in foreign television follows the pattern of operation of the medium at home. It has consequently been overwhelmingly commercial. Overseas enterprise by the television industry began ironically with RCA's sale of a transmitter to the Soviet government[1] in 1939, and has been growing steadily ever since. The sales by equipment manufacturers were soon followed by the spread of United States broadcasting methods (albeit not in Russia), and the direct involvement of private broadcasting corporations in the operation of foreign programming. Commercial television of American origin has not always been unanimously welcomed by people overseas, who may resent what some of them regard as a form of "cultural imperialism." But in the words of a vice-president of Time-Life Broadcast,

> The various underdeveloped countries are having to permit commercials because they can't afford a television system otherwise. . . . A man setting up a commercial station abroad has to be pretty sure he knows how to compete—and we have more knowledge in this field than anyone else in the world.[2]

The competition he mentions is presumably for entry into the broadcasting market, not in the day-to-day operation once broadcasting begins, for in this there is seldom much competition. The American companies have been able to convince their domestic market that commercial television is "free," and have clearly been able to convince at least the foreign licensing authorities that their own country can "afford" this style of operation too. There are of course real costs involved in "free" broadcasting, but these are diffuse and hidden (this is discussed further in Chapter 7). The United States government generally condones this overseas expansion by United States corporations but presumably for mercantilistic, not "free enterprise," reasons. For example, a past president of the National Association of Education Broadcasters has noted that, "United States law forbids granting a license for a television or radio station to a corporation in which there is foreign ownership."[3] The international television field is thus asymmetric due both to "natural" financial inequities and to the *laws* that govern broadcasting in the United States.

The success of American commercialism has been celebrated openly in the trade journals. Skornia illustrates this as follows:

> An editorial in *Broadcasting* magazine in March, 1955, told of the alleged victory of the American broadcasting plan, which has "prevailed in all democratic nations," over the so-called British Plan. The editorial concluded: "Henceforth the lexicon will change. It will be the 'American Plan' versus the 'Totalitarian Plan' until the latter collapses." Similarly, *Advertising Age* in November of 1959 observed that "nations that have not adopted commercial TV have made little progress." "Nations that have not resisted commercial TV have made rapid strides." The implication in such statements is that the United States commercial broadcasting system is finding a ready acceptance. Such is not the case,[4]

In Skornia's first source, commercial television is apparently assumed to have a monopoly of democratic virtue. Publicly financed systems like the British are labelled "totalitarian"! The second source implies that commercial television is causally related to national progress. This is at best a debatable assertion. It will be argued in later chapters that far from stimulating general "progress" a commercial network cannot even be shown to be necessarily helpful to economic growth. Indeed the evidence points to the contrary conclusion.

Private corporations are not the only North American influence on Latin American communications, so before outlining corporate activity in the region I shall briefly consider the effects of United States government agencies and foundations. The most important of these is the United States Information Agency, the specialized United States government organ for overseas communication. It is also the only United States government agency with a potential for regulating United States media corporations overseas. I shall therefore describe its operations first.

THE UNITED STATES INFORMATION AGENCY—
OFFICIAL VOICE AND REGULATOR

The first part of this section discusses the organization and official duties of the Agency. This is followed by an examination of the real and potential regulating powers that the Agency may employ to influence United States overseas media corporations.

The Structure and Official Function
of the Agency

The Agency was established in 1953 as an executive office of the government to coordinate previous official communications operations and to initiate new ones. In 1968, senior staff were given Career Foreign Service status, thereby giving the Agency employees parity with officials in the State Department.[5] The Director of USIA is responsible to the President and, with the approval of the Senate, is appointed by him. The current director is Frank J. Shakespeare, Jr., who was appointed by President Nixon in January, 1969.[6] The Agency's functions center primarily around the task of explaining government policies and American life to people overseas. Foreign policies are undoubtedly the most important of these. A Presidential Memorandum in 1963 outlines the Agency's role in this area. USIA should "help achieve United States foreign policy objectives by (a) influencing public attitudes in other nations,"[7] and (b) serving as an advisory and information source to policy-making organizations. To this end the Agency maintains liaison with the Department of State. The Agency must be consulted before any government programs affecting foreign media are begun. It is responsible "for the conduct of overt public information, public relations and cultural activities"[8] for all government agencies except the Department of Defense, which manages these tasks for itself.

It is often claimed by overseas nationals that USIA is a propaganda organ of the United States government. That is precisely what it is set up to be, and as such it has been quite successful. A former director, for example, has boasted as follows:

> I can report proudly that the exhibits, broadcasts, telecasts, films, books, pamphlets and periodicals produced by the U.S. Information Agency are now regarded as models by the Professionals engaged in the *arts and crafts of persuasion* [emphasis mine] .[9]

He follows this with a statement denying the existence of United States participation in a worldwide "propaganda contest"—he is only interested in "persuasion."[10] The difference is a significant one for the Agency. Under a succession of relatively enlightened directors, the Agency has tried to give an objective view of the United States and its policies and thereby retain a semblance of credibility. Within the confines of its official task it has generally done so and on occasion has incurred the wrath of other government agencies for its integrity.

The Agency has a staff of a little over 5,000 Americans, of whom 1,500 are serving abroad with the support of 6,000 foreign national employees. They work to achieve their information functions through most of the media channels available.[11] Stations overseas provide personal contacts, maintain libraries, and distribute subsidized books to schools, universities, and individuals. They also support "bi-national centers," which utilize the help of private United States citizens living abroad for educational (primarily language training) and cultural programs. There are 130 of these centers, most of which (110) are in Latin America. The overseas stations, known locally as the U.S. Information Service (USIS), also provide a six-day-a-week service to local newspapers and magazines, the basis of which is a 10,000 word radioteletyped release of United States news and commentary.

USIA is also charged with promoting all official large-scale exhibitions abroad, publishing magazines, and operating the Voice of America (VOA) broadcasting facilities. The VOA has 102 transmitters worldwide, which broadcast 932 hours per week in 36 languages to an estimated audience of 43 million people.[12] Magazine publications include the monthlies *America Illustrated* for Russia and Poland, *Topic* for Africa and the Near East, and two quarterlies for world distribution—*Dialogue* and *Problems of Communism.* In addition, the Agency runs a film and television service that will be described in more detail below. The operations and objectives are thus extremely diffuse and by no means simply fulfilled, given the Agency's staffing and budget limitations.

Until 1959, limited television activities were undertaken by the Voice of America. In that year a separate television project was inaugurated. In December of 1965, the television and film services were merged. This was a move to enhance efficiency, but more importantly, it appears, to save costs: 33 positions were eliminated and over $1 million "saved" during the following two years.[13]

The Film and Television Service produces and buys programs, which it distributes to approximately 2,000 television stations in ninety countries.[14] Unlike the VOA's radio activities, no transmitting stations are owned by the Agency.

The programs distributed by USIA may generally be classified as either "series" or special documentaries. In the former category, the most prominent is the weekly news series, "Washington Correspondent," produced in 14 languages for forty countries. The series is tailored for each country by the use of native commentators.[15] Another series, *Enfoque las Americas,* was produced for Latin America to publicize the Alliance for Progress.[16] Recent "specials" include the Spanish-language "Decisions: 1968," a documentary on the United States Presidential election, which was carried by television stations in 19 Latin American countries; "Richard M. Nixon: The New President," a thirty-minute film for television; and "Nixon: A Self Portrait," produced by CBS and acquired by the Agency for world distribution. Teletapes of United States space programs have been distributed by USIA, and a Yugoslav television team under USIA auspices was permitted to make its own documentary of space shots. (They also covered the 1968 elections.)

The major USIA responsibility today centers on the Vietnam war. JUSPAO (Joint United States Public Affairs Office), as the Agency is known in Vietnam, advises the military on matters of psychological warfare, and together with the Department of Defense, AID, and the Vietnamese Ministry of Information, was instrumental in setting up and operating the Vietnamese National Television Network.[17] The Agency in Vietnam is also responsible for non-military information to the world's media. To this end it gives press and newsreel releases, and sponsors and supervises foreign "guest" correspondents and visitors.

On a modest scale, USIA has also sponsored conferences on communications and engaged in training programs for overseas media employees. The 30th review notes that "The value of foreign journalists' and editors' tours of the United States has long been recognized; various exchange programs have encouraged and supported such visits, with USIA often sharing sponsorship participation with the Departments of State and Defense and other organizations."[18] A new program was launched in 1967-68, in conjunction with United States private radio and television companies, which brought ten journalists (four from Latin America) to the United States for a month's training at either a radio or television station.

Finances. It has been noted that the Agency is responsible for a large number of activities and must serve a rapidly expanding world communications network. As Table XI below illustrates, neither the size nor the growth rate of staff and appropriations seems to reflect this expansion. Indeed the number of employees has declined consistently during the last four years.

The government has claimed that complaints which imply that Latin America is neglected relative to other world regions are unfounded: On the contrary, it is argued, the region is given special emphasis. As evidence of this, USIA points out that its own allocations for the region grew from $17.9 million in fiscal year 1965 to $20.5 million in 1968.[19] But based on the total appropriations cited in Table XI, this in fact represents a *decrease* from 10.8% to 10.6% of the Agency's allocations. In fiscal year 1969, $11.6 million[20] (6.8% of the total) was allocated to the Motion Picture and Television Service. If Latin America receives a share of this proportional to its overall appropriation, then it can be estimated that a little more than $1 million will be spent on this crucial audio-visual medium in 1969. In terms of the high cost of television therefore USIA cannot be considered an important source of financing for the region's television, even though its programming and news services may heavily influence Latin American broadcasting.

The Regulatory Powers of USIA

The Agency is currently responsible for issuing export certificates for educational audio-visual materials and it similarly supervises imports of such material into the United States.[21] This gives the

Agency some regulatory authority over United States private communication organizations overseas. But most commercial material is still authorized by the Commerce Department, which is probably more concerned with increasing sales than ensuring the quality and suitability of our media exports. USIA is therefore *not* an overseas equivalent of the Federal Communications Commission. Rather, the Agency's former director interpreted its role as one of supplementing the image of the United States built around the activities and public relations of private expatriate corporations.[22] Indeed, this is the Agency's legal position: It is subordinated to United States private enterprise abroad by Congressional legislation that restricts its operations to those activities which do not compete with United States mass media corporations overseas. (Nor can the Agency compete at home: Its programs cannot be shown in the U.S.) This is not too great a constraint, however, because few of the commercial exports deal with "public affairs matters."[23]

Nonetheless there are areas of conflict between the Agency and private enterprise. The capacity of United States commercial television to fully represent United States *national* interests abroad has been questioned by Dizard.[24] A former writer-editor with Time, Inc., he was a career officer with the Agency prior to (and at the date of) his book's publication in 1966. His objections to the media corporations center primarily on the content and educational influences of their programming. In part, his criticism is due to a conflict over United States image building. USIA, he says,

> ... shows aspects of U.S. life which are intended to generate respect, admiration, and emulation of our democratic political system in other nations. For U.S. television networks and film companies to inundate these same nations with programs which do the opposite appears inimical to our total national objectives.[25]

Who is giving the most honest "image" is perhaps a matter of perspective, but it is clear that the corporations themselves are not unduly conscious of a public relations role—not, that is, one on behalf of the nation. Legally though, the total "image" field is theirs should they ever choose to exercise their option. But it should be noted that neither USIA ("image building") nor commercial television ("profitable operation") makes the economic development of foreign countries a major objective. Nor, of course, is there any reason stemming from their own organization imperatives why they should do so. The Agency in any case would be too weak to force the corporations to adhere to broad development guidelines even if it should formulate some. At present, however, the Agency shows no inclination to become active in development programs.

GOVERNMENT-SPONSORED AND OTHER INTERNATIONAL MEDIA ACTIVITIES

USIA has not been the only government agency involved with mass communications. This is particularly noticeable in the case of radio. Centered in Munich, Radio Free Europe was one of the first projects undertaken by the Central Intelligence Agency, when it was set in motion by Congress in 1949. In 1955 RFE was broadcasting to Communist Europe from 29 transmitters, primarily medium wave in Germany, but including a powerful short wave station in Portugal. RFE was set up as a private non-profit (tax deductible) organization which served as a rather transparent front for its CIA funding and the policy guidance of the State Department.[26] By 1956, RFE employed about 2,000 people: The Munich organization alone had a $3 million budget.[27]

Organizations similar to RFE were set up for broadcasting to other parts of the world: Radio Free Asia in 1952 for the Far East, using short wave transmitters in Taiwan and the Philippines, and Radio Liberation in 1953, which broadcast to Russia from German stations.[28] In the Western hemisphere, Radio Swan began its operation for the liberation of Cuba from its 50,000 watt station on Swan Island in 1960. Like the other stations, Radio Swan (later renamed Radio Americas) had its own civilian "front" office in New York, in this case headed—none too tactfully for Latin sensibilities— by a former president of the United Fruit Company.[29] Under alledgedly "absolute CIA control,"[30] the station played an intimate part in the unsuccessful Bay of Pigs invasion of Cuba.

Other national governments and foundations are also active in international communications. The governments of Britain, Germany, and France engage in operations similar to those of USIA through their own agencies—the Central Office of Information and British Information Services, Deutsche Welle, and OCORA respectively. UNESCO and the European Broadcasting Union (which sponsored international communications conferences held in Rome, 1961; Tokyo, 1964; and Paris, 1966) have been involved in the limited activities of "educational" television in developing countries. The Ford Foundation has also lent assistance to educational television projects. It is a co-sponsor of the Center for Educational Television Overseas, located in London, and has other projects in the Philippines, Argentina, and Mexico.[31] The Agency for International Development (AID) has rendered assistance to similar activities in Nigeria and Colombia.[32] But all of these efforts are small in terms of both impact and financial outlay, when they are compared with the overseas activities of the private media corporations. The operations of the latter are now outlined.

U.S. COMMERCIAL INTERESTS IN
LATIN AMERICAN TELEVISION

As in the United States, the three major television corporations—NBC, CBS, and ABC—are the dominant forces in television expansion overseas. A brief description of their activities and interests in Latin America, together with those of some lesser known corporations follows.

ABC-Paramount. This is by far the most active United States television corporation in the region. Its international division (ABC International) was formed in 1959, and the following year "advanced $250,000 to, and invested in, five Central American television stations . . . [which] became known as the Central American TV Network (Cadena Centro-Americana or CATVN)."[33] ABC is reported to own 51 per cent of this network.[34] In January, 1968, a similar network was formed in South America. It is called the Latin American Television International Network Organization (LATINO) and operates in six countries.[35] Both networks are part of ABC's "Worldvision" network, which the corporation describes as a "programming and advertising cooperative."[36] In addition, ABC also has ownership interests in some of the Worldvision broadcasting stations. By 1968, Worldvision operated in sixteen Latin American countries and in eleven foreign countries in other regions. It utilizes 64 television transmitting stations, which broadcast to an estimated audience of more than 20 million private households.[37] Given a high frequency of both public and private group viewing, the total audience (in persons) is therefore several times larger than this household figure.

NBC-TV. NBC's foreign operations are more limited than those of ABC. Its activities center on providing management and programming services to overseas networks. Thus NBC is the partner of the Nigerian government in that nation's television broadcasting. In like fashion, NBC has assisted in setting up new stations in more than twelve underdeveloped countries. But in addition to such aid, by 1965 the company had "direct minority investment in 13 overseas stations in 8 countries."[38] In addition, "NBC International deals directly with overseas broadcasters to sell NBC programs which are shown in 82 countries."[39]

In Latin America, NBC has given technical and financial assistance to television in Argentina, Mexico, and Venezuela. Investments have reportedly been "phased out" in all but Radio Caracas Television in Venezuela. NBC's major program sales office for the region is located in Mexico City. The office "dubs" the company's saleable domestic programs into Spanish and then distributes them throughout Latin America. The corporation also retains the services of an associated sales agent in Brazil.[40]

CBS. This has been the least active of the three major domestic television corporations abroad, perhaps due to its domestic success. In the early years of the medium, CBS helped set up commercial television in West Germany. It also has various partnership arrangements with "television centers" in Argentina,[41] and interests in production companies in Peru, Argentina, and Venezuela. The latter two are controlled by Goar Mestre, the ex-Cuban television tycoon, with CBS and Time-Life Broadcast owning 20 per cent each.[42] The company has also "held minority positions in broadcast outlets in Argentina, Venezuela, Peru, Trinidad and Tobago and the Leeward Islands."[43] It has also been active in cable television in Canada, Japan, Belgium, Australia, Mexico, and Argentina.

The president of CBS explained the paucity of overseas involvement relative to the other networks in the following manner: The opportunities for overseas expansion, he says,

> . . . just haven't been there as we define opportunity. We've had exploratory talks in South America—in Columbia, Brazil, Chile—but

they just weren't attractive opportunities. As you go around the world, television is either government or quasi-government operated and doesn't offer much inducement to invest. . . . We'd rather hold ourselves open for the total market."[44]

The less affluent American Broadcasting Corporation finds the investments worthwhile, but CBS apparently still enjoys a domestic bonanza. Obviously there is no consideration here of the overseas nation's development needs. The corporations are clearly profit-making institutions, not charitable organizations or long-term development agencies.

Other United States Interests. These are small when compared to the holdings of the domestic big three. The British program producing and contracting company, Associated Television (ATV), is the United Kingdom contractor for Musak (owned by the American *Jack Wrather Organization*). ATV and Wrather own one-half each of the British-based Independent Television Corporation, whose board chairman is predictably Mr. Wrather himself. The large investments of *Warner Brothers* in British television adds to these American investments.[45] But neither company appears to have expanded into Latin American broadcasting to date. United States companies active in the region include *Time-Life Broadcast,* which has interests in Goar Mestre's production companies in Argentina and Venezuela (with CBS) and in addition renders "technical and financial assistance" to two stations in Brazil. *Bartell Media* has a 60 per cent interest in two government stations in the Netherlands Antilles; *Wometco Enterprises* has station dealings in the Bahamas; *Caribbean Networks, Inc.,* in Panama and El Salvador; *Pan American Broadcasting Company* in Peru and Puerto Rico; and *Inter-American Publications* in three Puerto Rican stations. *Screen Gems* has joint ownership of one Venezuelan station and 100 per cent and 33 per cent, respectively, in two Puerto Rican stations.[46]

The penetration of the Latin American region's media has been effected by U.S. corporate enterprise[47] rather than by governmental or quasi-governmental agencies (as is the case with the British Broadcasting Corporation's activities around the globe). The cumulative effect of American commercial interests on programming in the hemisphere is clear even on a purely quantitative basis (see Table XII). It is greatest in the small countries and in Venezuela, Chile, and

Colombia (United States corporations have interests in 50 per cent or more of the programming stations in each of these countries).

The type of United States involvement varies from one country and station to the next, and possibly some involvements are not made public at all. In Central America, the ABC-Worldvision network, CATVN, has station affiliations in each country. The participating station in Costa Rica is partially owned (35 per cent) by ABC, as perhaps are other CATVN facilities. The Guatemalan Ministry of Education and the United States Information Service have cooperated with the CATVN Station in Guatemala City to provide some limited educational programming—from literacy drives to higher education—in the country.[48] Caribbean Networks, Inc., has interests in the second stations of El Salvador and Panama, where there are also Worldvision stations. Worldvision participates in the government station at Santo Domingo, and the single operation in Haiti. All three stations in Ecuador are affiliated in some fashion with ABC.

Of the larger countries it has been noted that three have heavy United States participation. One of the two state-controlled Colombian stations has Worldvision ties, and AID is assisting in a primary school educational TV project (modeled on the highly successful Italian "telescuola"[49] project) in the country. The Santiago and Valparaiso stations of the Universidad Católica in Chile both have Worldvision affiliations, although their emphasis until very recently has been predominantly educational. With the exception of Colombia and Chile, the predominant mode of operation in the region has been commercial, which has made United States corporate entry easier. This is most pronounced in Venezuela, where five of the six stations have ties with United States television companies. All of them are in Caracas. CBS and Time-Life each own 20 per cent of *Proventel,* a production company which also runs the Channel 8 station. NBC and Worldvision have interests in Channel 2, Radio Caracas T.V., which is repeated in Carabobo and Coro. Screen Gems is joint owner of Canal Once Television SA, and Venevision (Channel 4) is a Worldvision LATINO station.

In the remaining large countries, the United States corporate dominance is not so readily apparent. American interests, however, are concentrated in the largest urban districts and transmitting stations. Time-Life has invested approximately $6 million in TV-

Globo in Rio de Janeiro, Brazil, and also provides technical and financial assistance to TV Paulista in Sao Paulo. ABC has four LATINO stations in the preeminent Mexican commercial network, Telesistima Mexicano, and a production company in Acapulco. NBC has interests in XET-TV at Monterrey. The Ford Foundation has assisted some educational television efforts in Mexico, but clearly this is outweighed by United States commercial activities.

Holdings in Argentina, Peru, and Uruguay are numerically low, but they are also centered in the major cities. ABC has a LATINO station in Buenos Aires, while Time-Life and CBS each have 20 per cent shares in Proartel, the foremost production company in Argentina and the operator of Channel 13 in Buenos Aires. In Lima, CBS has ties with Pantel (production company and Channel 5), while the Pan-American Broadcasting Company has similar ties with Televisora America (Channel 4). In Uruguay, ABC has an affiliated LATINO station in Montevideo.

American influence on television is not limited to the formal station arrangements summarized above, although these are clearly of considerable strategic importance. Many of the programs and films shown on non-affiliated stations are of North American origin, news may come from United States news services (including those from USIA), and advertising may be accepted from American advertising agencies. Thus irrespective of station control, television in the region has a strong North American commercial flavor.

The way in which the American corporations listed above as active in Latin America conduct their overseas affairs is almost certainly influenced by their domestic operations, although they may possibly face more or (most likely) less regulation than at home. A brief account of the nature of domestic television will therefore be given in Chapter 7 before the effects of overseas operation are considered.

NOTES

1. W. Dizard, *Television: A World View* (Syracuse: Syracuse University Press, 1966), p. 155.
2. Sig Michelson in *Television Magazine*, October, 1966, quoted by J. Frappier, "U.S. Media Empire/Latin America," in *NACLA* Newsletter, (New York: North American Congress of Latin America), vol. 11, no. 9, January, 1969, p. 3.
3. H. J. Skornia, *Television and Society* (McGraw-Hill: New York, 1965), p. 186.
4. *Ibid.*, pp. 181-182.
5. USIA, *31st Review of Operations*, July-December, 1968, p. 23.

6. USIA, *Fact Sheet,* USIA Office of Public Information, February, 1969. Mr. Shakespeare has a strong background in commercial television. According to the *International Who's Who for 1969,* he worked for Procter and Gamble and Radio WOR, New York, prior to joining CBS in 1950. He served this corporation as General Manager of television stations in Milwaukee and New York, became a Vice President of CBS in 1963, Executive Vice President for CBS-TV stations in 1965. At the time of his appointment as Director of USIA he was president of the Service division of CBS-TV. In view of his occupational history, it seems unlikely that USIA will gain any regulating vigor in the immediate future. Not mentioned in the *Fact Sheet* was the fact that Mr. Shakespeare was also a key member of President Nixon's successful campaign team of 1968. See Joe McGinniss, *The Selling of the President 1968* (New York: Trident Press, 1969), especially chap. 3.

7. USIA, President's Memorandum, July 25, 1963, quoted in *The Agency in Brief,* 1969, p. 3.

8. *Ibid.,* p. 4.

9. Leonard H. Marks, USIA, *30th Review of Operations,* January-June, 1968, p. 4.

10. Of course *successful* propaganda results in persuasion. The Cold War, and what President Johnson referred to as "a battle for the hearts and minds" of the world's uncommitted, were patently propaganda struggles. Mr. Marks is here limiting the terms to persuasion that employs untruths rather than part-truths. See Dale Minor, *The Information War* (New York: Hawthorne Books, 1970), pp. 12, 40. For serious studies of propaganda, see Terence H. Qualter, *Propaganda and Psychological Warfare* (New York: Random House, 1962), and Jacques Ellul, *Propaganda,* trans. by Konrad Keller and Jean Lerner (New York: Knopf, 1966).

11. Information in this and the following paragraph is taken from USIA *Fact Sheet,* 1969.

12. The Armed Forces Network (radio and television), which came under direct military command in 1967, also broadcasts on a global scale. Ostensibly for U.S. service personnel, its "eavesdropping audience of foreigners [is] estimated at twenty times that of Voice of America English-language broadcasts." Charles C. Moskos, Jr., *The American Enlisted Man* (New York: Russell Sage Foundation, 1970), p. 101.

13. *30th Review of Operations,* p. 24.

14. Recent USIA pamphlet, undated.

15. *30th* and *31st Reviews,* pp. 11 and 5, respectively.

16. *30th Review,* p. 12.

17. *Ibid.,* p. 11.

18. *Ibid.,* p. 17.

19. *Ibid.,* p. 6.

20. *31st Review,* p. 26.

21. Executive Order 11311 (October 14, 1966) pursuant to Public Law 89-634, *The Agency in Brief,* p. 7.

22. Leonard H. Marks, *30th Review,* p. 37.

23. Dizard, *op. cit.,* p. 126.

24. *Ibid.,* especially p. 284.

25. *Ibid.,* p. 195. Another ex-USIA man, Don R. Brown, has taken issue with this point, but deals primarily with U.S. effects on *developed* countries. See his "The American Image as Presented Abroad by U.S. Television," *Journalism Quarterly,* Summer, 1968, pp. 307-316.

26. See Erik Barnouw, *The Image Empire* (New York: Oxford University Press, 1970), pp. 89-91.

27. *Ibid.,* pp. 103-104, For an account of RFE's role in the Hungarian uprising, see pp. 105-108.

28. *Ibid.,* pp. 91-92. For samples of Radio Liberation's programming, see pp. 170-173.

29. *Ibid.,* pp. 137, 146.

30. *Ibid.,* p. 187.

31. Dizard, *op. cit.,* p. 125.

32. *Ibid.,* p. 247. In Colombia, AID assistance consisted of the initial purchase of production equipment and 500 Admiral receivers totalling $577,000 in 1963. The

Peace Corps helps staff the broadcasting operation. By 1967, 347,000 students and 7,785 teachers were being served by 41 fifteen-minute programs a week produced for primary education. U.S. AID *Educational Television Project—Colombia,* Staff Reports (undated mimeo).

33. Frappier, *op. cit.,* p. 4.
34. Skornia, *op. cit.,* p. 187.
35. Frappier, *op. cit.,* p. 6.
36. Dizard, *op. cit.,* p. 64.
37. Frappier, *op. cit.,* p. 3.
38. Dizard, *op. cit.,* p. 63.
39. Frappier, *op. cit.,* p. 6.
40. Personal communication, NBC International, Ltd., May 28, 1969. A request for sales and investment figures was regrettably turned down in accordance with standard NBC policy.
41. Skornia, *op. cit.,* p. 187.
42. Frappier, *op. cit.,* p. 10.
43. Personal communication with CBS, July, 1971.
44. Merle S. Jones quoted by Frappier, *op. cit.,* pp. 7 and 11.
45. Skornia, *op. cit.,* p. 187.
46. Frappier, *op. cit.,* pp. 9-10. As of June, 1971, Screen Gems claims to have no station holdings. Their activity overseas is limited to program sales.
47. This has been studied in depth by Herbert I. Schiller, who wrote *Mass Communication and American Empire* (New York: Kelley, 1969).
48. Dizard, *op. cit.,* p. 234.
49. *Ibid.,* p. 233.

7.

institutional transfer: the united states tradition and the americanization of latin american television

In Chapter 6 it was concluded that North American interests and influences in the use of the television medium in Latin America centered primarily around the activities of the three major domestic corporations. Since their operations in the region are subsidiary to those at home, even though they may be financially important to the parent body, they are sure to be shaped by the corporate experience in the United States. For this reason the pattern of domestic experience is outlined in the first half of this chapter. The degree to which this is duplicated in Latin America by the major corporations (and in imitation of them) is the topic of the remainder.

THE NATURE OF TELEVISION
IN THE UNITED STATES

Several major features of the domestic television industry are claimed to shape the operation of the Latin American subsidiaries.

First, the industry is very new and its "bonanza" growth stage is only just showing signs of stabilizing. The medium is used primarily for commercial broadcasting of a uniquely American variety, and is only weakly regulated by the Federal government. Policy is apparently more responsive to increasingly complex corporate ties than to any real commitment to public service.

Television: The Bonanza Background

The United States was the first country in the world to introduce television on a mass scale. By May, 1964, 98.2 per cent of all American households had at least one set. Of these, 18.2 per cent were multiset households. There were an estimated 62,600,000 sets in use at this time.[1] The market for television sets is apparently close to saturation with new sets being sold primarily as replacements for earlier and defunct models. The demand for a second set in the household is almost certainly less pressing than it was for the first. This decline is reflected in recent production and sales figures (see Table XIII). The small increases in monochrome set production for 1965 and 1968 shown in the table, and (when we allow for a year or two lag) the continued surplus of sets produced over sets sold, are probably indicators of an expanding export market. Note that thanks to the introduction of color, total production has risen over the period covered, and it is consistently higher than domestic demand. The domestic sales figures for recent years show a large drop in monochrome receiver sales and an overall decline despite a steady increase in color set purchases. However, due to the much higher unit cost of the latter, dollar sales have probably continued to rise.

By July, 1969, a little more than 32 per cent of American homes had color television, up from 28 per cent the previous year, 20 per cent in 1967, and 12 per cent in 1966: There were an estimated 18.7 million homes equipped with color in mid-1969.[2] The proportion of these more expensive sets can safely be assumed to rise, but primarily as replacements for old monochrome sets. Thus despite the introduction of color, the industry is no longer experiencing the bonanza expansion that would be associated with a totally new product and virgin markets. This is apparent from the slowing color sales expansion, and from the decline in the total number of sets sold in the recent years compared to 1966 (as shown in Table XIII).

From the wide distribution of television sets in the United States, it is clear that the potential audience for transmitting stations is very large. Although television developed earliest in the Northeast region of the country, by 1956 most of the United States consumer market was served (more than 60 per cent of potential viewers in all regions). Large cities had the best coverage, but there was more than 60 per cent even in districts classified as "farm." Differences in coverage of national markets stratified by income, education, family size, age of housewife, or age of children were very small.[3]

The television set in each household was on for an estimated average of five hours and forty-six minutes per day in 1968, up four minutes from the previous year.[4] The time spent watching the medium is prodigious, but the annual increase is small and unlikely to grow rapidly in the future. The viewing audience increases throughout the day: "From an early morning level of less than a half million households . . . [it] climbs to about 15 million households at mid-day. The audience almost doubles between 8 and 10 PM."[6] This summary statement apparently applies to the estimated average audience in the early months of 1967. Summer viewing rates are significantly lower, especially in the afternoon and evening. This is clear from the audiences in January-February, 1967, and July-August, 1966, since potential audiences had not changed radically. Morning, afternoon, and evening audiences for the winter months were 7.4, 17.1, and 30.4 million homes, respectively. In the summer they were 6.0, 13.5, and 20.1 million.[6]

The United States Commercial Pattern

Television broadcasting in the United States has been overwhelmingly a commercial undertaking from the outset, although the airwaves are recognized by law, if not by those in the industry, to be public property. The Federal Communications Commission has therefore been given a weak regulating authority over the medium's operators, which consists primarily of the power to grant or refuse licenses to transmitting stations. "Interference" by the FCC in commercial operations is strongly resisted by the corporations, and public sympathy usually goes to the local men of the "public" corporation rather than to the government "intruders" from Washington. Indeed it is the government, as just another customer, that usually must follow the dictates of the networks. A striking example of this is the treatment of politicians, who as legitimate representatives of the "public" should presumably have some right of access to the "public" air waves. They do, if they buy broadcasting time. Otherwise they must be interrupted by advertisements like everyone else. Thus Dizard, although associated with USIA rather than a commercial network, has largely accepted the latter's broadcasting ethic. He was therefore shocked by the way that Castro could commandeer time on Cuban television. A young Cuban might be equally shocked to see the Vice President of the United States interrupted in mid-sentence for a commercial break.[7]

The triumph of commercial television is by no means "natural" or "inevitable." Governments in Europe, Canada, and Japan have managed to retain more regulatory powers, even though this often means that they must subsidize the medium. Britain and Germany, for example, both derive revenues for their support by imposing licensing fees on television receivers. Britain runs its own non-commercial network, while Germany limits advertising and prohibits the interruption of programs for commercial spots.

Public television in the United States is clearly no political match for commercial interests, and it lags behind its European counterparts. It is continuously short of capital and remains heavily dependent on private contributions. NET (National Educational Television) is further handicapped by the "Educational" label it carries. It is the largest non-commercial network and runs many cultural and general interest programs in addition to day-time school programming. Unlike their competitors, the public stations are openly expensive and require both tax money[8] and contributions. The burden of the latter, of course, falls only on those who contribute voluntarily. The widely held belief that commercial television broadcasting is "free" while public broadcasting is a luxury or liability is encouraged by the major networks. For example, the latter are opposed to Pay TV because they claim it would constitute the selling of public property, and deny the right of the individual owner to tune in "free."

Skornia has argued that commercial broadcasts are in fact by no means "free" to the consumer. There are, he says,

> many channels through which funds are secured from the citizen to
> pay for broadcast service. They are indirect, and they may or may

not be too high. They are, however, very real. They include what he pays for receiving equipment, installation, upkeep, and electricity or batteries; what part of the television-advertised products goes to pay for television time and talent costs [sic]; and various other expenses. . . .[9]

The receiver costs would presumably have to be borne under any system. Most of the broadcasters' expenses are met directly by advertising fees, but these, claims Skornia, are passed on to the consumer in the form of higher prices. The standard apologia for advertising—that it increases market size, which leads to subsequent economies of scale in production, distribution, and marketing, and hence lower consumer costs—is rejected by Skornia as a myth. He finds no instances of price reductions after any successful advertising drive. Good advertising means good profits for the manufacturer, advertising agency, television program networks, and stations. The latter, it may be noted, do not re-allocate the bulk of their surpluses to provide better public service, nor do they cut back on commercial spot sales. They do what any rational corporation does to benefit *itself*—they diversify and expand.

The networks program ostensibly "what the public wants." But it is unclear just who should be considered to constitute the "public," although to commercial spokesmen it is apparently the biggest majority at any given time. Nor is it readily apparent how the desires of the public, however defined, can be made known. Many program decisions are obviously made initially by the networks and their sponsors. The audience is only consulted, and this extremely haphazardly, after the program is aired. The networks thus constitute a far from perfect public forum of two-way communication. For example, "The Smothers Brothers," a peak time program that had run for two years on CBS, was summarily taken off the air in midseason. The reason for cancellation was publicly given as (minor) contract violations by the two producer-actors of the show and its declining popularity. But in private a CBS official gave a different reason: "One of them had been sticking his finger in the network's eye and something had to be done."[10] The show had used mildly liberal and minority themes, which CBS had been censoring for months on the grounds that the material would offend the "public." Although they usually adopt a posture of self-anointed champions of free speech, the networks nevertheless first look after their own interests and often behave capriciously as the above case illustrates.

Nicholas Johnson, a Federal Communications Commissioner, has openly described this type of behavior: The broadcasters, he says, are dedicated to "free speech for profitable speech only." Examination of the situations and issues "on which the broadcasting industry has raised the banner of 'free speech,' " he continues, "leaves one with the distinct suspicion that these occasions almost invariably coincide with the industry's monetary self-interests."[11]

Commercial television organizations broadcast from 662 stations (499 VHF, 163 UHF) in 1969 compared to 637 the previous year, 611 and 587 in 1967 and 1966, and 569 in 1965.[12] There is still therefore a limited station expansion, most of which can be attributed to new UHF transmitters. (For example, 7 new VHF and 44 UHF stations were added between 1967 and 1969.) The revenues of networks and stations have similarly increased every year since 1947, growing from $2,203 million in 1966 to $2,521 million in 1968. The early growth rates of more than 100 per cent per year, however, are now a thing of the past. Income (before Federal taxes) has also risen steadily from more than $311 million in 1962 to almost $493 million in 1966 and $495 million in 1968. A disproportionate share of this income was taken by the three biggest companies: In 1968 the three networks earned $56.4 million, their 15 owned and operated stations a further $122.4 million, while the remaining $316.0 million was distributed among the 622 independently owned stations.[13] Revenues to the networks came primarily from the sale of advertising time and programs to their owned and affiliated stations. The shares of individual networks in this revenue between 1965 and 1967 show that CBS is still the dominant corporation at home.[14]

Advertising Practices of Commercial TV

Advertising revenues derive primarily from personal and household consumer goods (see Table XIV). Between 1966 and 1968 there were some noticeable increases in product category expenditures among which cosmetics and laundry products were the most rapid growers. Confections, dental, and household paper products showed declines in television outlays. Overall, personal and household cleaning products increased their share of total expenditures at the expense of food and drink, and more precipitously, all other products. (See percentage figures for these three general categories in Table XIV.)

The conclusion suggested in Table XIV is that eating, drinking, smoking (until the recent ban on cigarette commercials), and cleaning are the main activities the advertisements promote (together they constituted 75.6% of all expenditures in 1966, and 77.6% in 1968); all are rather commonplace activities to be so heavily urged in the new "electronic" age over its most advanced medium. Of course everyone needs to do them and the market is truly a "mass" one for these products, so advertising is "justified." The nature of this type of advertising also means that it can be transferred overseas, since the products do not require a technologically sophisticated market. On the other hand, people can be expected to fulfill their basic needs without the urgings of advertising, although perhaps a few would be less well-scrubbed and over-fed. Competition is strong among the producers of these goods, but they apparently compete with each other through advertising rather than in the price arena. Some corporations, for example, those manufacturing detergents, carry this to the extreme of promoting their own ("rival") products against each other. The standard rationale for advertising—that it disseminates useful product information and therefore stimulates the market—does not seem to be the whole story in the case of such products.

The Regulatory Tradition: Television and the FCC

The mass media are regulated by a wide variety of government agencies. The basic guidelines have been produced by the executive branch and congressional legislation. On a day-to-day basis the Justice Department and the Federal Trade Commission have been involved with enforcing regulatory laws. But the most important agency in such matters is the Federal Communications Commission, which, as has already been noted, is specifically charged by the government with the task of regulating the electronic media. It has the authority to license stations, suggest broadcasting regulations to the United States Congress and Executive, and prosecute stations and networks for alleged violations of existing laws. The private industry, however, apparently has the upper hand in many of the disputes that are crucial to its operation. Due in part to its public image as the donor of "free" services and its powerful control of communications media themselves, it has successfully portrayed the FCC as an "intruding" organization that works *against* the public interest.

The weakness of the FCC relative to the private television industry could be attributed to collusion between the regulator and regulated as indicated by the interlocking of elite personnel. It is true, for example, that a retired Commissioner is admirably suited for lucrative posts in the private industries that he has "regulated" during his FCC tenure. As with other government officers, such changes in employment are not unprecedented. A few Commissioners may indeed have sometimes relaxed controls to keep open future employment channels. But such conflict of interest is difficult to prove and clearly does not apply to such outspoken Commissioners as Nicholas Johnson, whose remarks on the networks' self-interest have already been quoted.[15] The cause of the Commission's weakness therefore is probably not due to the doubtful integrity of Commissioners, but to the more basic structural defects of its organization.[16]

The FCC has a phenomenally wide range of duties in addition to its supervision of commercial television. These include a plethora of responsibilities (many of which are only vaguely defined) in all of the nation's sophisticated and expanding communications channels. These range from space satellites, telegraph and telephone use, to the protection of individual privacy in new "wire" connected computer systems; and from all public and private broadcasting to the licensing of pocket paging devices. In fiscal year 1968, there were more than 7,200 public broadcasting (radio and TV) stations in operation.[17] The Commission is responsible for the application of the "Fairness Doctrine"—the rules relating to advertising, political campaigning, and personal attack—in each of these stations. In fiscal year 1968, the Commission also prepared and held hearings on proposals to establish subscription television and to limit newswire contracts with broadcasters, in addition to fulfilling its more basic task of investigating a large number of cases of alleged programming and license violations. In most of these investigations it issued "warnings" to the offenders. Two licenses were revoked—the Commissioners' primary sanction—and 167 stations were given revocation warnings. But only a small fraction of stations (35 of the 7,200) were actually subjected to field investigations.[18]

The Commission had to fulfill these multiple tasks with a staff that averaged 1,470 employees and a budget of $19.17 million. This hardly indicates the dominance of "Big Government" in mass communications. Thus, for example, the commercial television companies (whose income was more than 20 times the total FCC appropriation) could therefore easily outstaff, outspend, and generally outflank the Commission on any matters where regulation might be in the public interest, but at the same time would greatly inconvenience the corporations. Obviously, then, despite the good intentions of the FCC, its structural weakness—resulting from its low budget and staff together with its poorly defined authority—is such that commercial television in fact goes virtually *unregulated.*

Corporate Ties and Public Service

The major networks are not autonomous, entrepreneurial establishments in any real sense. NBC is a subsidiary of RCA as are Hertz, Commercial Credit Company, Random House, Sunbury and Dunbar Music, and Defense Electronic Products; while CBS's "family" is reported to include Holt, Rinehart & Winston, Creative Playthings, Baily Films, and the New York Yankees[19] baseball team. ABC-TV and its international divisions are part of the greater ABC-Paramount organization, which is in turn linked to Gulf Western. A further merger with International Telephone and Telegraph Corporation (ITT) proposed in December, 1965, was forbidden by the United States Department of Justice early in 1968.[20] Even so, it is apparent that all the networks have commercial linkages or interests that extend beyond public broadcasting.

In summary, the corporations that are most active overseas are also dominant TV corporations at home. What is considered "natural" at home is therefore expected to be duplicated elsewhere. This includes the ideology of "free" commercial television, programming for mass markets, time priority for advertising, and resistance to regulation. Alan Thomas has pointed out that each television viewer has three distinct roles: As *audience* he wants to be entertained and indulges himself; as *market* he is open for a sale; but as *public* he rationally dictates what he needs for his own good. In Canada, he explains, the

> public strongly supports the Canadian type of broadcasting although as *audience* many of the same people may watch television programs from United States Stations along Canada's borders. The Canadian

Public is very Canadian. The Canadian *Audience* and *Market* are essentially American—very much like the people of the US in the same roles.[21]

United States television at home, with minor exceptions, serves audience and market. As will be demonstrated, it is fitted for—and in fact follows—the same pattern abroad.

THE AMERICANIZATION OF LATIN AMERICAN TELEVISION

The presence of major corporations in Latin American television has been documented in Chapter 6. It is not assumed here that such foreign enterprises necessarily constitute barriers to the region's development merely because they are not indigenous. This is the crude anti-capitalist or anti-imperialist position for which there is little scientific evidence. Nor is it agreed, as McLuhan has argued, that the television medium itself is in any way inherently damaging. Instead it will be argued that program content, the linkages with advertising and United States consumer manufacturers, and the strong commercial nature of the operations in general, are each contributing factors which fashion the medium into a powerful conduit for widespread consumerism. This is not offset by pro-ducerism imperatives in the medium—the promotion of skills and consumer tastes suitable for goods that are widely attainable—nor by increased productive capacity. Given this consumerism/producerism imbalance, the medium in itself is probably detrimental to the internal development of the region, although many other factors, including the existence of bonanza enterprises, undoubtedly mask its effect on the economy as a whole.

The initial purveyors of commercial television often claim that their operations will produce significant social and economic benefits. But like the exhortations of the would-be opium merchant, their claims are not always recognized by foreign countries at their face value, even though the disadvantages of the medium are not so readily apparent until after the enterprise is in full swing; that is, if the disadvantages are ever recognized at all. Nonetheless, since the "benefits" are not totally convincing, it is sometimes necessary to use considerable persuasion in order to attain market entry. Skornia, for example, concludes that the pressure tactics employed by United States firms in England were instrumental to the establishment of commercial channels in that country "... over the objections of large segments of both political parties, and without the British public having any real opportunity to participate in the decision."[22] Trade journals, advertising agencies, and broadcasters, he concludes, are openly proud of such manipulative "successes."

The Triumph of Commercial Television

Unlike Europe in the early days of the medium, public television has not gained any substantial foothold in Latin America.[23] Thus all of the countries have predominantly private and commercial forms of operation, even where the government has either been active in the past, or is still active in broadcasting. The Mexican government, for example, showed an early interest in the medium. But today Mexico has only one public station—that of the Instituto Politecnico Nacional—among its 24 programming stations.[24] Chilean broadcasting was originally government owned and non-commercial, but the Universidad Católica operations in both Santiago and Valparaiso are now commercial stations with ABC Worldvision affiliations. The Venezuelan Ministry of Communications runs one educational and cultural station, Televisora Nacional, but the remaining five are all commercial with United States corporate interests in each. Peru has a similar public station under the Ministry of Education, and the Brazilian government owns Televisão Nacional, the only non-commercial station of the 33 operating in Brazil. Radio-Televisora Nacional in Colombia and T.V. National in Guatemala are both government stations which nonetheless carry private advertising commercials. (In Colombia the government leases one national channel and one limited to Bogota to commercial programmers.) Thus public non-commercial television has not taken hold even in the countries where the government operates stations. In the remaining countries, television is entirely commercial and is privately owned.

The nature of this broadcasting has a direct impact on the two factors that have been isolated as crucial to development, producerism and consumerism.

Television and Consumerism

In Chapter 6 the United States holdings in the region were outlined. It was noted that there were North American interests in each country, although their extent varied from country to country. Influence, however, is apparently wider than financial holdings alone. Two Latin Americans have expressed this in their report to UNESCO ·as follows:

> Throughout the continent the television stations are directly or indirectly dependent upon the major United States networks—and the greater the need for the latest technical equipment and trained technicians, the closer those links are. In Latin America the United States has a monopoly of the supply of the new technology, the basic film material, the technical experts and, of course, the large-scale capital needed to increase the size of the local investment.[25]

Their last sentence, as they probably realize, is an exaggeration. Latins are themselves active in financing the medium and some native interests, for example, Goar Mestre's operations, are even international in scope. The indirect influences are nonetheless very real. These include the importation of programming materials and the widespread imitation of United States practices by indigenous program producers. This is clearly apparent in local programming and advertising practices.

Programming. The programs shown on overseas television, particularly in Latin America, are often of United States origin whether or not the United States has station or network interests in the country. In 1965, for example, program sales of United States television programs abroad were alone worth nearly $80 million.[26] In the same year it is estimated that the United States television industry as a whole earned $125 million in overseas sales (programs, equipment, and other services). These earnings are thought by Dizard to be highly significant for the following reason: "For some parts of the television industry—notably the production of television films—the overseas market means the difference between profit and loss on its operations."[27] As in the United States, old movie films are also sold to the Latin American stations. These and their similarly old television counterparts are sold for widely fluctuating prices. Such re-usable products have often already recouped their costs on the domestic market or been written off as losses, so business is very lucrative and (arbitrary) pricing becomes a matter of good will and contract skills. With the rapid worldwide expansion of stations and audiences, the film companies have to date enjoyed a "sellers' market."

As mentioned previously, the major United States networks also have production company interests in Latin America. Even so, approximately 80 per cent of the hemisphere's current programs—including "The Flintstones," "I Love Lucy," "Bonanza," and "Route 66"—were produced in the United States.[28] Within the limits imposed by foreign governments, including their ability to set quotas on imported programs, the network interests usually stimulate such United States imports. Thus, for example, when the Central American CATVN network was formed, ABC International announced that the stations "would carry film shows from United States firms; this included ABC-TV, which itself owned and exported such programs as 'The Untouchables.' "[29] ABC's interest in the larger LATINO network to the South probably gives similar prerogatives.

The suitability of these programs (which constantly depict North American life styles and folklore) for poor Latin countries is open to serious question. As an avid educational television proponent and intra-industry rival, Skornia is harsh in his questioning of their suitability:

> Isn't the world we live in today so literally *one world* that we can no longer be indifferent to poverty, hunger, and misery anywhere on the globe? And what effect on starving people do our programs have—featuring waste, dissipation, violence, and luxury?[30]

One possible answer to his question would be that the effect of this type of programming is to encourage an elite sector to live in North American style without the sacrifices necessary for indigenous development, while the masses are shown—but cannot enter into—the modern cosmopolitan world. The content of such programs undoubtedly influences the viewer toward consumerism, without upgrading his productive skills or increasing his willingness to save and sacrifice.

Although there is an extensive and viable research literature on the misanthropic effects of various types of television programs, the major companies either ignore or discredit the findings. The usual ploy is that the viewer will not learn from, or imitate, the contents of an "entertainment" program—a fallacy clearly exposed by McLuhan.

The governments of several developed countries—including France, Germany, and Japan—now regulate program content to deemphasize crime and violence and to enforce safeguards for the young. The FCC is far less potent in the United States, and even its mild brand of regulation is resisted by United States corporations abroad, where of course the Commission itself is not authorized to act.

Programming, then, is generally similar to that in the United States, even when the material is produced indigenously. It is geared to the "audience" and "market," and its object is primarily to entertain the viewer and to sell the goods it advertises.

Advertising practices. The overseas programming prerogatives of the networks extend to, and often coincide with, those in advertising: "For example, ABC can sell *Batman* to an advertiser and then place *Batman* along with designated commercials in any Worldvision country where the advertiser wants it to appear."[31] Advertisements carried in this way are usually for the goods of sophisticated, or at least large-scale international, corporations which are predominantly North American. They sometimes use the same advertisement for their product that is used in the United States after it has been dubbed in Spanish. The product, however, is destined for the Latin American elites, not the mass middle class as in the United States. Even when the advertisements give accurate consumer information of the products (which they patently do *not* in the United States), they do not usually serve any viable *mass* needs when transferred intact from the United States to an underdeveloped country.

The scheduling of advertisements throughout the region usually follows the United States pattern. Thus the programs are frequently and consistently interrupted for commercial spots. The options demonstrated by Japanese and some European commercial stations—that is, placing advertisements *between* programs or scheduling them all at the end of the day's broadcasting—are not exercised in the region. The emphasis is thus heavily on sales. Indeed, ABC International's LATINO chain (and CATVN, which is now treated by the corporation as an integral part of it) is not described in the trade as just an interconnected programming network. Instead, it is billed as "... basically a sales tool, offering advertisers discounts as well as the convenience of a multi-station buy through a single source."[32] This clearly favors the international corporation ("discounts" given to large buyers run as high as 25 per cent, and only the large enterprise needs such "multiple buys") over the emergent indigenous manufacturer. Thus the style of advertising appears to promote cosmopolitan sectorism; that is, it serves the interest of international consumer-good manufacturers who cater to local "modernist" elites.

Television and Producerism

Although the emphasis of the medium in Latin America is clearly on the sale of "modern" sector goods, it cannot be assumed that it has no part in facilitating producerism. But if we discount the impact of the limited educational programming, producerism is not being consciously or directly promoted. Rather, the rewards for sectoral inequality are being displayed, but the means to attain a more widespread material culture are not. The producerism effects that remain therefore stem from minor information services and the indirect effects of the programming.

In a media study conducted by Deutschman and his associates, respondents were questioned about the usefulness of the media for providing information relevant to their tasks as (technical) change agents. They rated television and radio equally, but both media rated very low: "The mean rating fell about midway between 'little' and 'some' useful information."[33] Meteorologists and air traffic controllers found reports on the weather useful, and public officials used news broadcasting to gauge public reactions to their agencies' activities[34] (actually what they were probably getting was the *stations'* reaction); this is not a direct indicator of public reaction, but merely one of the possible sources of influence on it.

The same team of researchers also reported on some of the indirect influences of seemingly innocuous "entertainment" types of program:[35] A personnel director, for example, claimed to use television dramas as case studies in his training program on personnel problems. Street and office scenes shown in television films were found of value (but surely a limited one) to a city planner in Nicaragua and a Colombian office manager. A bank manager helped defend his enterprise by following television programs on fictional bank robberies; and police in Panama, Peru, and Honduras picked up police methods from watching crime dramas. (No doubt the local criminal elements also learned a little from such programs.) But these indirect effects that may have minimally improved efficiency are clearly minor when compared to the producerism potential of the medium, and they are almost certainly far outweighed by its consumerism effects.

NOTES

1. *U.S. Bureau of the Census,* sample survey of 26,000 households, conducted in May, 1964. Quoted in tabular form by H. J. Skornia, *Television and Society* (New York: McGraw-Hill, 1965), p. 90.
2. *International T.V. Almanac* (C. S. Aaronson, ed.) (New York: Quigley Publications, 1968, 1969 and 1970 editions), p. 26A.
3. Leo Bogart, "The Growth of Television," Table 3, compiled from Market Research Corporation reports, in Wilbur E. Schramm (ed.), *Mass Communications* (Urbana: University of Illinois Press, 1960), p. 108.
4. The figures for 1965 and 1966 were five hours 29 and 32 minutes, respectively. See *International T.V. Almanac,* 1968 and 1970 editions, both pp. 26A.
5. *Ibid.,* 1968, p. 26A.
6. *Ibid.,* p. 26A. The 1970 Almanac lists January-February, 1968, audiences as 9.3, 19.1, and 29.0 million homes for the same viewing periods. This indicates audience gains in the morning and afternoon over previous years, but a loss of prime time evening viewers.
7. This happened with no subsequent public comment on NBC's nationally broadcast "Tonight Show," April 21, 1969. It was not an isolated occurrence. President Nixon, however, has been a prolific user of pre-empted television time.
8. The recently founded Corporation for Public Broadcasting is grossly underfinanced. The original Carnegie Corporation Commission recommended a sum of at least $100 million per year, a sum about the equivalent of the CIA-funded radio stations. The 1968 requested appropriation for CPB was $4.5 million. See Erik Barnouw, *The Image Empire* (New York: Oxford University Press, 1970), pp. 193-195, 339.
9. H. J. Skornia, *T.V. and Society* (New York: McGraw-Hill, 1965), p. 90.
10. *Time Magazine,* April 18, 1969, p. 65.
11. N. Johnson, quoted in *Ibid.,* p. 65.
12. *International T.V. Almanac.* All statistics in this paragraph are from the 1968-1970 editions, pp. 20A-26A.
13. In 1966 network earnings and those of their stations were $78.7 and $108.1 million, respectively. The other 593 stations shared $306.1 million between them. See 1968 *Almanac,* pp. 20A, 22A.
14. Computed from data in the 1968 and 1970 *Almanacs:*

	% of Total Network Revenue		
	1965	1966	1967
ABC	27	28	27.5
CBS	39	39	39.0
NBC	34	33	33.5

15. See also his book *How to Talk Back to Your Television Set* (Boston: Little, Brown and Co., 1970).
16. The following paragraph is based on information given in Federal Communications Commission, *The F.C.C. in Fiscal 1968—A Summary of Activities* (Washington, D.C.: FCC, 1968).
17. The number of private stations numbered 1.7 million. These are licensed by the FCC as "Safety and Special Radio Services." They include police, military, aircraft, industrial, and marine transmitters.

18. This excludes the inspections of field engineers. They made 12,000 inspections of radio stations in fiscal 1968, 1,500 of these in the "Broadcast Services." They found more violations of regulations than the total number of inspections.

19. Frappier, *op. cit.*, p. 6.

20. *Ibid.*, p. 3.

21. Alan Thomas, *Audience, Market, Public: An Evaluation of Canadian Broadcasting,* Occasional Paper No. 7, University of British Columbia, Department University Extension, April, 1960. Cited in Skornia, *op. cit.*, p. 122.

22. Skornia, *op. cit.*, pp. 11-12. The British affair is given full treatment in W. W. Wilson, *Pressure Group: The Campaign for Commercial Television* (London: Martin Secker and Warburg, 1961).

23. This applied to the seventeen countries in my sample. Cuba, which I have excluded from consideration throughout, has been an obvious exception in the post-revolutionary years.

24. Station information given below was gathered from sources in Table IX, Chapter 5, and UNESCO, *World Radio and Television* (Paris: UNESCO, 1965).

25. Luis P. Estrada and Daniel Hopen, *The Cultural Value of Film and Television in Latin America* (Paris: UNESCO [Mimeo], July, 1968), p. 6. This, they claim, leads to the lamentable stagnation of the region's arts and the "Americanization" of Latin culture. They are not directly concerned with television's implications for consumer styles and economic growth.

26. According to the Motion Picture Export Association, the 1965 telefilm sales overseas amounted to $76 million. They reached $80 million in 1968. See Erik Barnouw, *The Image Empire* (New York: Oxford University Press, 1970), p. 309.

27. Dizard, *op. cit.*, pp. 3-4.

28. Frappier, *op. cit.*, p. 2. In the summer of 1970 the following U.S. programs were broadcast in Colombia: "That Girl," "Marcus Welby," "High Chaparral," the "Jerry Lewis" and "Carol Burnett" shows, and "The Untouchables."

29. Skornia, *op. cit.*, p. 187.

30. *Ibid.*, p. 191.

31. R. Tyler, "Television Around the World," in *Television Magazine,* October, 1966, p. 33, cited by Frappier, *op. cit.*

32. *Advertising Age,* Jan. 29, 1968, p. 53.

33. P. J. Deutschman et al., *Communication and Social Change in Latin America* (New York: Praeger, 1968), p. 65.

34. *Ibid.*, p. 65.

35. *Ibid.*, p. 65.

8.

television and united states investment, advertising, and sales in latin america

If the North American style of television broadcasting is indeed an important carrier of consumerism, there should be a close relationship between the television capability of a country and the consumerist nature of its economic behavior. The degree of United States corporate control of the medium is only one indicator of this consumerist style because of the widespread (but not easily measurable) extent of imitation employed by domestic media operators. But the distribution of the television audience (as measured by the number of sets per 1000 persons), if we assume fairly uniform commercial programming from one country to the next, should be more closely indicative of consumerism. An intermediate variable here is the type and amount of advertising beamed to the viewer.

ADVERTISING IN LATIN AMERICA

Like the electronic media, the advertising industry in the underdeveloped world has also been expanding much more rapidly than economic growth as a whole. Although the volume (and of course potential market) is much lower than in "developed" countries, the rate of growth and profit of poor country agencies is higher. Between 1960 and 1964, for example, advertising volume was up 26 per cent in fourteen major industrial countries, but 50 per cent in eighteen "still developing" countries (Colombia, Costa Rica, Ecuador, and Peru were included in this group). Income was up 26 per cent in the former group, 35 per cent in the latter.[1] This trend has probably continued.

Unfortunately, despite the efforts of the International Advertising Association, accurate and comparable national figures are not available for advertising volume in many of the world's countries. In Latin America, total volume figures are not comparable from one country to the next due to different reporting methods. Table XV, however, shows specific media billings that were reported in a reasonably uniform manner. Since the U.S. accounts for more than half the world's advertising activity, the Latin countries are of course far below North American levels. But as Table XV shows, advertising is generally growing faster in the Southern hemisphere: Thus Argentina, Colombia, and Chile experienced extremely high rates of expansion. Mexico and Venezuela, however, both reported declines; indeed, in Venezuela the declines were precipitous. In all of the countries except Colombia (where radio was marginally the leading grower) television was the most favored medium, showing either the largest gain or smallest loss of the three main advertising channels.

When controlled for population size, these media expenditures put some Latin American countries among the world's leading advertisers, even though the absolute expenditures look miniscule when compared with those in the United States. In 1968[2] the U.S. led per capita radio advertising statistics with $5.67 per person. Of the remaining countries Chile ranked seventh with $1.20 and Colombia eighth with $1.01. Mexico, Brazil, and Argentina ranked 7th, 8th, and 10th, respectively, in total radio billings. The Latin American region was also well represented in national television advertising ratings for 1968. Brazil ranked 6th, Mexico 8th, and Argentina 9th in total TV expenditures. In per capita terms Argentina was 10th with $2.77 spent per person, while Venezuela followed in 13th place with $2.05. Thus by world standards Latin America is by no means a "backward" region for advertising activity.

Table XVI gives a breakdown of expenditures in the three leading media categories for those countries in the region for which data were available. Television was the most favored advertising medium in four of the seven countries (Peru, Venezuela, Brazil, and Mexico, in which TV's share reached or exceeded 45%).

In every Latin country listed in Table XVI the combined electronic media, radio and television, carry a larger share of advertising than is the case in the United States. They are very clearly already the *leading* advertising channels in the region. (In every country they account for more than 50 per cent of expenditures.) The countries that spend the least on television advertising (Chile and Colombia) also have the lowest distribution of the medium.[3] As the number of TV sets expands, the television share of expenditures will undoubtedly increase, since programming is now commercial and Americanized in both countries. North American companies have interests in one of the two Colombian stations (the other is government-owned but commercial), and two of the three in Chile.

ADVERTISING AGENCIES–UNITED STATES LINKAGES

The rapid expansion of television in the region, and the concurrent growth of television advertising in the sixties have both been characterized by foreign penetration. The growth of the medium, as has already been documented, was accompanied by United States corporate penetration. The North Americans had the investment funds, programs, technical competence, and experience that were required to run viable commercial television stations. The same combination of finance and expertise has similarly opened up foreign markets for United States advertising agencies.

The expansion of United States advertising agencies into overseas markets has been very rapid. Indeed, according to spokesmen for the trade, advertising is one of the leading enterprises in international expansion: "The figures leave no doubt that when it comes to participation in the world economy, advertising is among the most forward looking of business fields."[4] This growth is apparently still increasing. Edward L. Bond, Jr., the Chairman of Young & Rubicam, is presumably well qualified to assess future investments in the advertising industry. He comments on this growth as follows: "I think that the proliferation of American agencies abroad will continue to rise at a rapid pace. . . . US advertising agencies opened 48 new offices abroad last year [1967] setting a new high in international growth. I feel certain this trend will continue."[5] Bond's own company and the other established major United States agencies have taken the lead in this expansion.

Since 1967 the pattern of international expansion appears to have changed from one of founding a wholly owned or majority branch to one involving partnership arrangements and mergers with established agencies overseas. This seems to apply both to established international agencies and to later entrants. Thus D'Arcy, which has a Mexican branch, merged with McManus, John and Adams, and together with the European Intermarco chain has formed the DMI international group.[6] Ogilvy and Mather have acquired holdings in five Latin American countries since the end of 1969. The agency gained "substantial minority" interests in Standard Propaganda of Brazil (the country's third largest agency) and Corpa, the largest agency in Venezuela. Together with its 40 per cent share of the third-ranking agency in Argentina and interests in Mexico and Colombia, it is now an advertising power in the Southern Hemisphere.[7] Two other U.S. agencies have bought into two British chains that are active in Latin America and around the globe: Leo Burnett bought the major agency portions of London Press Exchange, and Sullivan, Stauffer, Colwell and Bayles (SSC&B) now holds a 49 per cent interest in Lintas.[8]

Of the 55 agencies in the United States with billings of more than $25 million in 1967, 32 were active in international advertising. In 1970, there were 60 agencies above this billing level, 40 of which did business overseas including 24 of the top 25 agencies.[9] The domestic and overseas billings of the top ten agencies active overseas and six others which have operations in Latin America are shown in Table XVII. International billings are clearly important to many of the large American agencies. For the biggest three, J. Walter Thompson, McCann-Erikson, and Young & Rubicam, international billings accounted for 34.5, 37.5, and 21.4 per cent, respectively, of their total billings in 1966. For all three, the international portion of their billings has been increasing. In 1970 their foreign components were 43, 55, and 31.5 per cent. Some smaller agencies do an even larger proportion of their business abroad. Eight of the sixteen agencies listed in the table recorded a greater absolute expansion (or in the case of two, a smaller decline) overseas than at home between 1966 and 1970. Overseas activity therefore is not just a marginal operation but an undertaking that is vital to these agencies.

The greatest expansion of advertising agencies overseas is predictably not in underdeveloped countries, whose markets are far less lucrative, but in the developed countries. Most of the advertising billings abroad therefore represent activity in Canada, Europe, and Australasia. Nonetheless, there is significant activity in Latin American countries, especially in services related to the "premature" or leading medium, television.

The Latin American stations reportedly do most of their business with American Advertising Agency subsidiaries that sprung up in response to the new media, expanded world trade, and direct United States private investment in the region.[10] Table XVIII lists the major agencies active in the region. It is clear that these are by no means marginal operations. With the exception of Quadrant and Marplan —which are specialized overseas operations—and Coordinated Communications, they all reported more than $40 million in total billings in 1967 and 1970. In addition, the three biggest agencies on the United States domestic market are well represented in the region. The expatriate agencies therefore undoubtedly have regular United States clients and established broadcasting outlets, consisting primarily of the "big three" networks. Nor, as has been noted already, must they necessarily have offices in the country in order to place advertisements in the media. The Worldvision sales network encourages multiple station (and nation) buys. These agencies, of course, also serve native manufacturers who wish to place television advertisements.

The agencies listed in Table XVIII do not always operate under their domestic names in Latin America, so the number of offices and billings include data for agencies listed elsewhere[11] as their overseas branches or affiliates. With the exceptions of Kenyon and Eckhart, Compton, and Coordinated Communication, all of the agencies in the region followed the general growth trend in business activity reported for overseas agencies as a whole.[12]

The *Advertising Age* survey indicated the financial strength and dominance of United States advertising on the global scene. This is made explicit in the survey report itself:

> One of the most significant aspects of the overseas picture is the very large presence of U.S. owned agencies in other nations. Whereas native admen of other nations have made their influence felt in advertising and advertising techniques, both in their own countries and occasionally here at home, U.S. capital and techniques have made a major impact on advertising around the world.[13]

The overall dominance holds true for the Latin American region as Table XIX indicates. Many of the agencies could not be positively identified as domestic or foreign, so the degree of foreign influence is understated. Nonetheless, it is clear that the United States agencies have a strong foothold in the region.

Table XIX shows that United States activity in Latin America is considerably greater than all other foreign countries combined. In addition, with the exception of the Mexican-owned agency in El Salvador, none of the (non-United States) foreign agencies was the largest in any of the Latin American countries in 1968. With the sale of London Press Exchange to Leo Burnett and the Lintas-SSC&B merger, foreign competition was virtually eliminated (see number of foreign agencies for 1970 in parenthesis). In 1968, North Americans had interests in half or more of the major agencies in nine of the sixteen countries. Two years later all but two countries had more U.S.-owned than domestic agencies, and in one of these, Argentina, the four largest billing agencies were all U.S.-owned or affiliated. This financial dominance characterizes most of the countries in the region. Thus in 1968 a U.S. agency was the leader in nine of the countries. By 1970, three more domestic leaders had been supplanted by U.S. agencies. Indeed, most of the agencies positively identified as subsidiaries of United States companies are either near or at the top of the total billing listings for the countries in which they operate. As their numbers grow and as they move up in the rankings, U.S. influence increases. Agencies in Venezuela and the Dominican Republic have already become wholly U.S. operations: The trend illustrated in Table XIX, if it continues, means that more may follow. Thus there can be little doubt that the United States style of advertising is dominant in the region.

The leading agencies are heavy users of the television medium, despite the relatively small audience size. For example, J. Walter Thompson, the largest agency in Argentina, does more than 40 per cent of its business in that country with the television industry. Other leading agencies there spend from a little more than 20 to over 70 per cent of their total expenditures on the medium. Local industries, as well as developed country exporters, are interested in placing their advertisements on the television screen. Indeed, one agency noted that its Brazilian clients spend proportionately more than their American counterparts on television, as opposed to other forms of advertising.[14] They are more cosmopolitan than the foreign "moderns." The American agency, however, is overseas primarily to provide services for its chief customer, the American consumer goods manufacturer.[15] Local manufacturers using the television media for advertising are probably either American and other foreign subsidiaries, or "modernist" domestic companies that cater to sectoral consumerism.

The natural advertising and consumer goods linkages—the ties between established North American agencies and their clients —clearly mesh well with their habitual outlets, the television corporations. The presence of all three United States interests in the region serves to emphasize the fact that the structure of United States television operations in Latin America is geared to business, not developmental, imperatives. Their prime responsibility is a good yield for their stockholders and expansion. They do this in the manner that has been so successful in the United States—by stimulating consumer goods sales—with the same business partners. The effect of this is to channel Latin American wealth into the American international corporations. These, rather than the nation state (as in Britain's early industrial dominance), become the "world's workshop." In this fashion, the avowed intent of the Latin American countries to industrialize is undermined.

The United States government verbally argues that the long-term United States public interest will be served by universal economic development, and USIA attempts to act in—or to buttress—this belief. But the appointment of a Sears Roebuck director as Under-Secretary of State for Inter-American Affairs and United States co-ordinator for the Alliance for Progress,[16] indicates that the government may still equate corporate experience (Sears Roebuck, for example, has extensive consumer goods interests in Brazil, and United Fruit's interest in the region is well known) with public wisdom. Similarly, given the magnitude of the Rockefeller holdings in the region, the commissioning of Nelson Rockefeller to study the development problems of Latin America was another stunning indicator of corporate policy dominance. The final report,[17] however, recommended a diffuse array of humanitarian measures as is customary for government reports. These include steps to improve health, education, and welfare in the region. There should also be an effort to improve communications, including the upgrading of the Voice of America to make it "at least competitive with Radio Havana"[18]—as if U.S. commercial dominance of the media didn't already exist!

When it comes to economic recommendations, the mission's report runs truer to expectations, and it is probably these suggestions that will be most heeded. At no point is it intimated that these policy goals might *conflict* with the laudable humanitarian ones. (Military programs, which might also conflict, are not dealt with at all.) One of the overall "national policy objectives" is that "the U.S. should provide maximum encouragement for private investment throughout the hemisphere."[19] The central problem here, says the report, "is the failure of governments—to recognize the [undemonstrated] importance of private investment;" instead they fear U.S. corporate domination and exploitation,[20] views which the report without any supporting evidence labels "mistaken." To aid the private investor it was proposed that there be no U.S. tax on foreign income, but that losses could be tax deductible.[21] Somehow humanitarian and developmental concerns have receded into the background here. Instead it is simplistically assumed that what's good for the U.S. corporation will also aid the Latin countries. It is argued below that this is an invalid assumption.

UNITED STATES TRADE AND INVESTMENT
IN LATIN AMERICA

Direct investments of North Americans in the region are apparently related to United States media interests, but the relationship is not a simple one. Clearly the type of investment and the varying constraints on media development and penetration modify any simple linkages. Table XX shows United States investments and television availability by economic level for 8 Latin American countries. Total United States investment in these countries is not highly correlated (rho = .64) with the availability of television audiences, but this is perhaps because extractive investment, for example, in Venezuelan oil, does not require a local market. Manufacturing investments, however, are highly correlated with the number of television sets in use (rho = .97), with only Mexico (where a very high proportion of total advertising is done on television) falling out of order (one rank). United States interests in television stations and advertising agencies, as demonstrated in Table XX, are clearly well represented in all four top investment countries.

The relation between United States manufacturing investment and the existence of television advertising facilities geared to a large audience (or market) is clear from the correlation of this investment both with television size (rho = .97) and with Gross National Product (rho = .98 for the eight countries in Table XX). Total United States investment, as would be expected, is not highly related to market size as indicated by GNP (rho = .71) or television availability (rho = .64).

The presence of United States manufacturers in the region apparently sets up pressures for a duplication of the television advertising support given at home, and the United States companies which provide these services are therefore encouraged to enter the foreign market. The investments of the latter will probably meet resistance to penetration in proportion to that experienced by the manufacturing investor. Conversely, where sales facilities already exist, United States manufacturing investment may be encouraged, and the marketing "infrastructure" becomes the "leading" or causal factor. However, once both are well established, as they appear to be already in the larger Latin American countries, they may be considered mutually supportive. Both are prime agents of consumerism—the manufacturer typically produces sophisticated goods, and the media services market them in the countries' modern sectors. This type of product, as opposed to mass goods aimed at the basic needs of the population, normally demands considerable marketing expenditures. The assertion that United States manufacturing investment is of this consumerist type is strongly supported by Table XXI.

The manufacturing component of the Gross Domestic Product [Column (3), Table XXI] for the five countries for which data were available is taken as an indicator of indigenous manufacturing sales. It is not highly correlated with the advertising expenditures shown in Column (1): The correlation coefficient for these two variables (Pearsonian r) is .80. United States manufacturing investment, however, is related much more strongly to advertising. For Columns (1) and (4), the value of r is .99. Assuming that United States manufactured goods have a consumerist effect in Latin America and that (like the goods made in the region by the overseas United States corporations) they require considerable promotional efforts, a high correlation between Columns (1) and (3) would be expected. This, however, is not the case (r = .60), in part because the import values include all types of goods, and therefore probably mask the effects of consumer goods alone. But the weakness of the relationship is primarily due to the low import figure for Argentina. This is almost certainly not because the Argentine economy is resistant to consumerism, but because it relies more heavily on Europe than the other Latin countries.[22]

The relationships found between United States enterprise and advertising channels have been limited to those countries—primarily the most affluent ones—for which data were available. But they probably also hold for the countries excluded. The consumerist manufacturer can advertise his goods on television in any of these countries through channels familiar to him at home. As an added convenience, multination buys are possible through the ABC networks. True, television is still scarce in the poorer countries and audiences are small absolutely, even though they greatly exceed the size that would be expected for countries at their economic levels. Nonetheless, the commercial structure of television stations is established and the necessary advertising facilities are already there. Pressures toward consumerism can therefore be expected to grow with the expansion of the television audience throughout the region, and in the process this will strengthen the tendency toward modern enclave formation and economic dualism.

NOTES

1. International Advertising Association, *Advertising Investments Around the World—The Five-Year Trend* (New York: International Advertising Association, October, 1965).
2. International Advertising Association, *World Advertising Expenditures,*1968 (New York: IAA, 1970), pp. 19, 22, 23.
3. As indicated by the number of receivers per 1000 people. See Table IX for 1967 figures.
4. *Advertising Age,* March 31, 1969. That this should be the case perhaps indicates that consumerism is the main thrust of U.S. private investment overseas.
5. *Advertising Age,* March 25, 1968, p. 118.
6. DMI announcement in *Advertising Age,* March 29, 1971, p. 43.
7. See *Advertising Age,* July 20, 1970, p. 4; January 4, 1971, p. 49.
8. *Ibid.,* January 4, 1971, pp. 46, 49.
9. See data sources of Table XVIII.
10. In 1950, $4.4 billion; in 1966, $11.5 billion. Frappier, *op. cit.,* p. 2. This will be examined in more detail below.
11. *Standard Directory of Advertising Agencies* (Skokie, Ill.: National Register Publishing Co., Inc., No. 157, June, 1969). The directory lists one office each of J. Walter Thompson and Young & Rubicam, four of Marplan, and one or more offices of seven other North American agencies in Latin America that do not appear in the *Advertising Age* survey.
12. The 746 agencies listed in the *Advertising Age* survey reported billings totalling $5.9 billion in 1970. The 691 reporting for 1968 billed $4.8 billion, and 616 agencies covered in 1967 registered $3.7 billion. *Advertising Age,* March 31, 1969, p. 1; and March 26, 1971, p. 1.
13. *Advertising Age,* March 31, 1969, p. 16.
14. C. McMillan, R.F. Gonzales, and L.A. Erickson, *International Enterprise in a Developing Economy,*(East Lansing: Michigan State University, Bureau of Business and Economic Research, 1964), p. 152.
15. According to J. Frappier (p. 2), U. S. exports of merchandise to Latin America in 1967 were worth $4.1 billion.
16. Charles A. Meyer was appointed to these positions by President Nixon on March 10, 1969. To take the post he resigned from the boards of Sears Roebuck, Dow Jones, Inc., The Gillette Co., United Fruit Co., and the Philadelphia National Bank. I am not questioning Mr. Meyer's integrity nor his competence here, but noting that among candidates with Latin American experience, business expertise was apparently the most valued.
17. Nelson A. Rockefeller, *The Rockefeller Report on the Americas: The Official Report of a United States Presidential Mission for the Western Hemisphere*(Chicago: Quadrangle, 1969).
18. *Ibid.,* p. 139.
19. *Ibid.,* p. 89.
20. *Ibid.,* p. 89.
21. *Ibid.,* pp. 89, 93.
22. In 1967, 23 per cent of Argentina's imports came from the United States. The North American share was considerably higher in the other countries: Mexico 64 per cent, Venezuela 50 per cent, Colombia 48 per cent, and Chile 39 per cent. AID, *Latin America—Economic Growth Trends,* Table 15, p. 27.

9.

conclusions

This chapter deals first with the conclusions to be drawn from the empirical study of Latin American television, and then its relation to the earlier discussion of consumerism and to communication theories of development. Since the television data at least partially confirm the view that consumerism is a prime obstacle to development, other (non-communications) variables that are conventionally linked to development are briefly re-examined in terms of the development thesis expounded here. Emphasis is on the political dimension, which affects not only the control of the media, but economic life in general.

THE DEVELOPMENTAL USES OF
TELEVISION IN LATIN AMERICA

In Part I, the concepts used in the investigation of development were examined and found to be generally unsatisfactory for describing the social and economic changes taking place in the Third World. These concepts, for example, seem to be inadequate to explain the cosmopolitan sectorism that characterizes these countries, the sameness that welds the cities of developing countries into a single financial and technological unit, a global metropolis. The limited concept of consumerism was proposed to focus attention on the institutionalization of "modern" cosmopolitan life styles. Producerism is a wider concept that attempts to put various activities that lead to the alleviation of mass needs under one heading. It includes organizational factors, but avoids treating all mechanization (industrialization) as necessarily serving these ends. These two concepts were claimed to be applicable at both the societal and the individual levels. It was hypothesized that they are intimately related to the formation of material wealth.

Communications theories of development were also examined. It was concluded that the development of the media does not automatically lead to economic growth since both producerism and consumerism elements are introduced simultaneously. A growth environment is dependent upon the mix of these elements in the media. Communications are nonetheless important to developing countries because they are potentially a "leading" sector; that is, media development can take place in poor countries, and indeed has done so extensively, before they reach the economic level or stage associated with such media growth in the histories of the more affluent countries.

Part II attempted to trace the developmental uses of the most advanced medium in Latin America. Throughout the region the media in general, and television in particular, are more widespread than would be predicted from economic levels. This is in itself an indicator of the region's sectorism and consumerism. Television and its advertising support system are clearly dominated by U.S. interests in both the financial and the stylistic senses: The North American pattern of operation with a few minor modifications has been adopted throughout most of Latin America.

Consumerism and Television

Latin American broadcasting was found to be strongly influenced by United States practices, due both to imitation and to the widespread presence of the major North American broadcasting institutions in the region. The domestic operations of these United States corporations are claimed to be devoted almost entirely to consumerism (sales and entertainment). In Latin America the television broadcasting stations are functionally linked to United States manufacturers through branches of major United States advertising agencies. This activity is not claimed to be conspiratorial, nor does it account for all television activity. But this transplanted United States style of operations is a major force in shaping broadcasting as a whole. Advertisements encourage the consumption of foreign-made or imitated products; they do not encourage asceticism and personal savings habits, nor are they likely to stimulate the production and sale of indigenous mass products in the "traditional" sector.

Like advertising, the program content in the region is also predominantly North American in origin or influence. If we infer that programs depicting "modern" life styles shape the aspirations of the viewer, then program content also has consumerism effects. Although most of the viewers are in the wealthier income groups, the medium is increasingly gaining a mass audience due, in part, to communal viewing but also to the growing availability of cheap "used" receiver sets as the most affluent buy their second set and discard their old "obsolete" ones. Unfortunately this audience increasingly consists of people whose incomes are generally insufficient to keep pace with the new aspirations induced by television.

Producerism and Television

Adherence to the United States broadcasting style has led to a neglect of possible producerism uses of television; the medium in Latin America is therefore used primarily as a sales and entertainment rather than educational instrument. As such, it is often argued, it stimulates productive activity by creating material "needs"; that is, it breaks down non-materialistic traditionalism. But this is only an indirect way of fostering producerism and is less effective on the poor who already have fairly obvious experienced "needs." The economic imperatives for stimulating demand may be valid in an "affluent" economy, but are of value only in the "modern" sectors of underdeveloped countries. True, as the Deutschman study discussed in Chapter 7 demonstrated,[1] a few bankers, policemen, and government functionaries can pick up some minimal information from entertainment programs that proves useful in their work. These, perhaps, constitute indirect producerism effects. But the *direct* use of the medium to induce producerism is rare. Indeed, such use appears to be less in Latin America than in the United States—the developed country with the *least* extensive use of the medium for "educational" (for example, skill training) purposes.

The United States government has engaged in some television operations overseas that take developmental needs, as well as the public "image" of the United States, into account. The experience gained in various domestic educational TV projects and materials from them have been useful to those in the underdeveloped countries who have contemplated the introduction of educational television. Unfortunately, as the Colombian case illustrates, the emphasis on ETV in these countries often subsides when the transmitters and sets arrive and operating costs begin to climb. The Latin American governments thereafter usually adopt the standard United States view that ETV is a luxury, while commercial TV is free.

Some formal educational programs overseas have been underwritten by American foundations and the government, but clearly the wider possible public uses of the medium have not been financed or even examined seriously by the donors of aid.[2]

Many underdeveloped countries urgently need "agricultural, medical and educational instruction, which TV could provide." "Must they," asks ex-NET president Skornia, "huddle night after night around television sets watching United States westerns and crime and adventure series?"[3] So long as the "modern" cosmopolitan sector (which of course includes those who make the society's key decisions) continues to receive extensive outside support for maintaining and improving its life style, "they"—meaning the poor segments of the audience—presumably must also.

But the potential of the medium remains. It demonstrably could promote literacy (the "Telescuola" literary drive in Southern Italy is the outstanding model for this), and numerous productive (and, indeed, recreational) skills could be taught. For those who feel morally bound to provide the masses with a primary or even secondary education, television can help break the depressing cycle of scarcity by relieving teacher shortages. That is, if it is not used merely as an "enrichment" for already well staffed schools, as is usually the case in developed countries. Public health projects could also use the medium for the dissemination of information.

Even the consumer could be better served by intelligent product information rather than by seductive advertisement. In the words of a prominent educator, it would then "inculcate habits of rational choice and decision"—the functions of a teacher—rather than "irrational and impulsive choices." He concludes that

> —the teacher's job is to encourage intellectual and moral self-discipline; the job of the advertiser of consumer goods is to encourage self-indulgence.... So basically the advertising profession and ... the teaching profession are at odds with each other.[4]

To fulfill its development potential, television must be a teacher. It must teach skills that can be used to produce the basic needs of the mass population in these underdeveloped countries. They need low-cost housing, school, clothing, and food, not the slick but relatively useless products that so much of television programming promotes.

The producerism emphasis must be in proportion to the growth that is needed. If mass communications are to be a tool in achieving growth rather than a mere reward (often prematurely and to only a small part of the population) for it, simple imitation of the most successful Western "educational" practices will not be enough. Achieving the 5 to 6 per cent "sustained" growth rates of the developed countries is a difficult but still too low a target for the poor countries' aim. If global economic inequalities are to be reduced, the "underdeveloped" countries must grow much faster, especially if their populations continue to grow so rapidly.[5] Producerism must therefore be actively promoted to an unprecedented degree and consumerism must be inhibited—the exact reverse of present usage of the mass media in Latin America.

Implications

Latin American countries, although there are variations among them, demonstrate how *not* to use television for developmental purposes, assuming rapid *national* economic growth to be a prime goal. Alternatively, television may be seen as providing benign circuses in lieu of improved livelihoods for the bulk of the population; as a sop to keep the modern sector "happy," or at least trapped, in a sophisticated but relatively stagnant and culturally parasitic part of the cosmopolitan market. If the government wants growth, then it cannot afford the "free" services of alien corporations over which it has no effective long-term control, no matter how persuasively the corporate salesmen sell their wares. If the medium is to be used to encourage producerism, it must be effectively controlled.[6]

The same order of implications applies to the United States government if it really desires the rapid development of poor countries, above the short-term pecuniary interests of its corporations. The Federal government has devoted only half-hearted efforts to regulating the media at home (through the FCC), and even less to the control of United States media companies in Latin America. In fact, even in its main function of "image" building abroad, it is generally acknowledged that USIA has been far less influential than the overseas United States corporations. It has almost no regulating power over North American media interests abroad. Both public regulating agencies function on low budgets and staff and in these terms are far weaker than the United States corporations with which they must compete. Both agencies (or perhaps just the FCC if its regulatory powers were extended beyond our national borders) would have to be strengthened if more developmental use of the electronic media is desired.

There has been some recognition by the United States government, even though perhaps only fleeting, that "what's good for General Motors" is *not* necessarily "good for the country" as a whole. And yet the parallel notion that "what's good for ABC is not necessarily good for Guatemala"—even if this is perhaps more obvious—is far less readily accepted by the American government and public.[7] If the United States government is really concerned with its national image abroad and the viable development of foreign economies, it should perhaps maintain at least as much control over the United States corporation abroad as it does at home. International relations are anarchic enough already. The growth of international (in reality, stateless) corporations can only further complicate global affairs.[8]

The United States government could therefore help promote the developmental use of overseas media by curbing the consumerism activities of the United States media corporations, or at least not objecting to their indigenous regulation. But it is unlikely to do either with any enthusiasm. A more positive approach might be to actively encourage the developmental use of the mass media overseas. The Peace Corps' educational television project in Colombia was a step in this direction. Even if programs must be geared to the local audience, the United States can usefully provide the technical skills and hardware necessary.[9] If the media become widely recognized as potentially very powerful devices for promoting development, perhaps the financial inhibitions apparent in the Colombia project may be overcome.

United States efforts in this direction could be channeled through a national agency for overseas media development that could draw on the resources of NET, FCC, and the private media industry. A clearinghouse for worldwide media research findings would also be invaluable. Such an agency could cooperate with the existing apparatus of the United Nations concerned with mass communications. UNESCO[10] has compiled extensive documentation in this area. It has also pioneered the spread of educational television, and conducted training programs for media personnel (for example, the Latin American Centre for Higher Studies in Journalism, at the University of Quito).[11] Like most United Nations projects this branch of operations has long been underfinanced. Perhaps now is the time both to supplement these activities and to provide them with more funding as an investment capable of rich returns to mankind.

CONSUMERISM THEORY AND NON-COMMUNICATION VARIABLES

As Chapters 1 and 2 illustrate, there is a wide range of development theories built around both macro and micro concepts. The consumerism theory outlined in Chapter 3 and utilized in the media chapters does not necessarily invalidate these often conflicting theories. Rather, it directs attention to the possibility that the key explanatory variables chosen by different theorists—urbanization, technology, education, and so on—may not have a direct and unitary effect on economic development. Consumerism and producerism may be intervening variables. The plethora of development theories has generated several important variables of this type. They will be given a brief consideration here, since each has policy implications for any development-oriented government.

Urbanization. The concept of urbanization is taken to be a purely ecological one. It has two main elements: the absolute growth of metropolitan (high-density population) centers, and the growth of these centers relative to the non-urban population. There are social repercussions to this massing of population, but the concern here is only with its relationship to development.

The frenzied, active aspect of big-city life is commonly remarked upon by even the casual observer: The city is "where the action is." Effort is also assumed by most scholars to be best mobilized in an urban setting. African cities, for example, have been characterized by their generating, communicating, innovating, and integrating functions.[12] In those countries that cannot afford the luxury of freeways and garden cities, it can also be noted that the bulk of non-agricultural production is done in large cities. In short, producerism can be greatly facilitated by the process of urbanization. Many urban centers retain a basically industrial character—the "drabness" of Pittsburgh, Manchester, or the Ruhr cities, of Osaka and perhaps Hanoi—but urbanization also provides the setting for consumerism as the cosmopolitan nature of many cities indicates. Indeed, some cities may be almost entirely devoted to this brand of modernism, as are, for example, Las Vegas and Miami and some tourist and "fun centers" overseas.

Much of the West's consumption drive is made in the cities of the Third World, and many become predominantly modern in this sense. Horowitz, for example, has noted that the "Peruvian cities preserve their commercial, administrative, and military features and remain *centers of consumption* instead of bases of production" (my italics).[13] As earlier chapters demonstrated, the commercial media also emanate from the cities. This beachhead of consumerism usually sets up demands for more of the same—more cars, gadgets, and maybe imported foods and clothing. Accompanying demands for such things as highways, electric power,[14] and the amenities provided by the tertiary (service) sector, are usually granted because they are the demands of those in power. In a weak economy, however, they represent a gross waste of scarce resources, and add to or perpetuate the inequalities in the society. The influence of "modernity" in the city is not limited to the elite consumer; even the labor unions can be seduced by it, as shown by their preoccupation with the maintenance or slight betterment of their standard of living. Urbanization, then, can either aid or impair economic growth. But widespread consumerism and the development of a parasitic tertiary (service) sector[15] apparently leads primarily to the less desirable outcome.

Education. Nobody who accepts the idea of human capital can deny that educational facilities and practices have an effect on development. But as one education expert has warned, we should not make it a "panacea to correct all deficiencies."[16] Then, too, there is the unsettled problem of priorities within educational systems: the dilemma of deciding whether the expansion of primary or higher level education will be most beneficial, and whether vocational or general education[17] is most conducive to development.

There can be no doubt that education at all levels can be vital to producerism as I have defined it. Increased education—which is difficult to achieve in rapidly growing populations—may lead to greater instrumental capacity (the human elements by upgrading job and administrative skills). If this capacity can be used, economic growth is enhanced. The educational system may also transmit nationalism, which will be a positive developmental factor if it includes an ascetic work-oriented ideology.

The consumerism effects of education, however, must also be considered. The schools and universities may instill unrealistic material "needs," and equip the student with job skills more suited to technologically advanced countries. Thus we often see surplus lawyers and, perhaps more tragically, engineers in the unemployment statistics of underdeveloped countries. These may emigrate to the West, where their material expectations can be met and their skills utilized; even though these individuals may benefit, in most cases spectacularly, their emigration is a great loss of potential human resources for the poor country.[18] In addition to instituting consumerist attitudes, the very prominence of the school in poor countries may be a consumerism factor, for palatial educational buildings, like other prestige public works, are a sign of Western affluence rather than indicators of any real commitment to the fulfillment of educational imperatives.

Technology. The role of technology in development has already been mentioned. Using more productive tools and power sources was seen as one way, but certainly not the only method, to enhance producerism. In the "advanced" society, whose material and human resources are utilized relatively fully, growth may rely heavily on technology. Wellisz has documented this quite well: "The amount of man-purchased capital and the rate of capital formation play a more important role in development than the primary resources." But, he continues,

> more than two thirds of the increase in national income that occurred in the United States over the last 90 years is attributed to technological change [presumably including skills] and only one third to the increase in capital and labor.[19]

This does not, however, validate the technological determinism of, for example, Richard Meier,[20] Robert C. Wood,[21] and other scientist-engineers, even though their one-sided approach to development is both understandable and, to a degree, useful. Clearly, capital formation and existing resources limit the degree to which new technologies can be implemented.

The kinds of technology that will lead to economic growth are *not* in fact immediately obvious. Wellisz,[22] for example, has outlined two common approaches to this problem that he finds unsatisfactory: (1) Adopting the newest available technology. This has an emotional (what I would call a "consumerist") appeal and is claimed by its advocates to be a competitive and viable response to free-world market conditions. But as Wellisz notes, such technology often has a low impact on employment, the scale of operation that it dictates may be too big to be practical, and its adoption will obviously exacerbate the country's sectoral imbalance. Even on purely short-run economic grounds, modern technology has to be adapted to different "factor proportions" including, for example, a cheap labor. Unfortunately, these factor proportions are usually ignored in the training given to foreign students in the West; such training is usually geared to specific Western conditions. (2) The other approach is described as "retracing" the Western path, which assumes that the "stages" of growth experienced by developed countries must be repeated by the "latecomers." This, says Wellisz, fails to take into account the changed world context of development. It rules out the development of finished goods for export, and the benefits to be gained by "skipping" steps. To avoid the shortcomings of these two approaches, Wellisz advocates the gearing of technology to local conditions. It might be added that it is the *material* conditions, not the "consumer" oriented desires of the elite population, that are important here.

To facilitate the application of this "local" approach, there is a vast need throughout the Third World generally for research and development centers. The obstacles to both their establishment and their successful operation are many. There is of course a large literature, produced in the main by anthropologists and rural sociologists, on the problems of technological diffusion. One of the often unstated obstacles to guided diffusion stems from the fact that it is usually confirmed "moderns," both technologists and administrators, who run these innovation drives. They may be ashamed of their country's "backwardness" and opt for a few prestige institutions that compare fairly well with those in the developed West; institutions through which they can build an international reputation in their professions. Unfortunately the United Nations has recommended the development of this "modern" type of institution even in poor African countries.[23]

Perhaps the consumerism effects of such advanced research centers outweigh their net yield of producerism. Clearly their very presence means that interest in technology that can be widely applied in the poor country and which necessitates working in the "bush" with primitive equipment and low rewards, is an "irrational" aspiration for the bright young student scientist. If he is doubtful of reaching the very top scientific echelon, of getting a position in the modern research center, he will wisely (for him) switch to the study of law, secure a position in some government bureaucracy, or emigrate.

Trade and Aid. Contrary to the commonly held view that financial ties with the West contribute to economic growth in the poor countries, the theory developed above suggests that existing relations in fact inhibit growth. Both trade, which makes the latest Western goods available, and aid, which may influence the choice of development projects, represent external pressures toward consumerism. The simple textbook view of the mutual benefits of trade—the law of comparative advantage—has been seriously challenged. The actual traders involved may benefit mutually, but the nations as a whole may not. The widely propagated thesis of Raúl Prebisch has claimed that terms of trade are controlled by (or at least are in favor of) the finished goods producer. The supplier of raw materials is faced with declining prices relative to manufactured consumer imports.[24]

Trade, of course, could be used to obtain machinery and tools geared to the local economy and thereby facilitate producerism. Unless such orders are willingly filled by the developed countries, trade of this nature would probably be *between* less developed countries. But this is seldom the case. Similarly, aid could be used for productive purposes that have more than a merely symbolic "modernizing" impact. It is a source of external capital investment, and should be subject to the same "rules" of wise utilization as "private" investment; that is, it should be allocated for the good of the national economy as a whole. Due to the poor uses to which aid is so often put—prestige projects and military equipment—it may in fact benefit the donor more than the recipient. Since the former often stipulates that the "expenditure" must be in the form of goods from the donor country, the aid amounts to forced (on donor nation's taxpayers) purchase of domestic goods in the rich country. No doubt this stimulates the donor's economy. The benefits to the recipient's economy will depend on the *nature* of the goods.

Even if we discount the above reservations on the nature of aid, the *quantity* of aid is small and relatively declining. This is illustrated by Table XXII. The poor countries will clearly not catch the rich because of the latter's charity. The United Nations target was for a 1 per cent Gross National Product outflow from the rich nations to the poor,[25] a modest amount hardly expected to yield short-term parity. Of the major developed countries listed in Table XXII, only France has consistently surpassed this target, and until 1968 its contribution had been continually diminishing. The United Kingdom and United States have both been reducing capital outflows, the latter in 1968 ranking equal lowest (with Italy) among major donors shown in Table XXII. Germany and Japan have increased their contributions throughout the decade.

The Latin American region as a whole, however, does not appear to have benefited greatly from these capital outflows from the developed countries. Indeed, as Table XXIII indicates, the hemisphere has itself experienced a net outflow of capital in recent years. The largest economies, Argentina, Brazil, and Venezuela, experienced a net outflow in 1967 and 1968. They were joined by Mexico and Peru in the latter year. Chile and Colombia both reversed their deficits of the previous year in 1968, perhaps a hopeful sign for future development. But the overall outlook is not very encouraging. The claims of some Latin Americans—claims derided by the Rockefeller mission—that the developed countries "take out" more than they "put in" appear to be justified.

The Political Dimension

The development problems of the less developed countries are clearly monumental. It has been argued that the massive urbanization that many of these countries are undergoing is not an automatic solution to their problems, nor is it a simple expansion of Westernized education or technological diffusion. Finally, they cannot realistically expect the developed countries to provide sufficient financial aid to spark and sustain their development. Their solutions must therefore stem from within and must include both an outpouring of productive energy and a downplay of consumerism— the alien material style that distorts their economies.

In the face of well entrenched external commercial pressures and the widespread co-optation of their population to modern life styles, it appears that effective development imperatives can be implemented only by imposing strong political controls. Even then, the task would be extraordinarily difficult. A developmental government must fight off the cultural invasion, while rediscovering or inventing a new indigenous culture; it must also devise an alternative incentive system to replace that currently provided by "modern" consumer durables and the reductiveness of life in the exclusive cosmopolitan sector. The limited steps that could be taken to convert the use of the mass media to developmental ends have already been discussed. The more general implications of the consumerism theory for growth-oriented political leadership will now be outlined.

Spengler[26] has outlined what he calls the "essential political conditions" for development. These require a degree of mobilization and integration that is apparently lacking in most Third World military regimes and democracies alike. They include:

(a) *minimum public services*—law and order, education and public health, money and banking, a legal structure for business, and the encouragement of foreign investment;

(b) *growth stimulation*—tax structures that encourage private investment, productive government expenditures, encouragement of entrepreneurs by a decentralized economy, support of basic research and technology, infrastructure underwriting, development planning, control of inflation, independent agencies for reviewing the government;

(c) *personnel* placement and upgrading; and

(d) the development of *political instruments*—one[27] or at most two political parties committed to development, and the meeting of welfare demands.

Spengler seems here to want the best of both worlds, a free enterprise (but government-supported) system in which the masses are integrated into compliant political parties. With the exception of the latter condition, it is an outline of what the stagnating polities actually do already, the setting for neocolonialism and uneven sectoral growth. The contradictions in the formulation are readily apparent. How can mass consensus be gained when the rich get richer (with aid from the tax structure), while the masses serve as a reserve labor force amicably suited to the fluctuations of an unplanned (or partially planned) economy? How can mass compliance be gained for no cost; that is, while welfare spending is kept to a minimum? The scheme is a blueprint, albeit unwittingly, for mass suppression and the free exercise of anti-humanistic private gain. Political mobilization to induce an ascetic-productive ideology is necessary for capital formation, but in order to work it must apply to the *whole* society, not just the unprivileged masses.

In his critique of the Prebisch thesis, Gomez[28] argues along these mass democratic lines. Rather than the slow social and political integration of the population into the modern, urban culture (as Spengler's work and the assumptions of those who advocate the consumerist brand of modernity imply), he argues that the whole population must be included before real economic growth is possible. Unlike Prebisch, his political views lead him to reject existing power holders as growth agents. To him they are "reactionary," and cannot effect growth. Recent events in Argentina, Brazil, and to a lesser degree Mexico, give some credence to his claim, but the new Peruvian and Bolivian regimes may demonstrate that reform from the "top" is in fact possible. Chile under Allende may be the first test case for development incorporating the needs of the masses in its planning.

Whether one insists with Gomez that revolutionary mass mobilization or mass reformist pressures are the political prerequisites of growth, his call for national integration seems valid enough. By this he means mass political participation and economic integration (presumably increased welfare and government expansion of employment) that would permit a stronger role for the government. Although the overall economy would not immediately benefit, the government would then have more *internal* legitimacy. External retaliation for economic nationalism of this type could range from a cut-off of aid and credit—which given their past record of ineffectiveness might perhaps be a small price to pay—to outright intervention, subversion, and invasion. Such a government, if it is able to avoid internal or external military action, could enforce the sacrifices and planning that Gomez argues are required for growth. The crucial problem which he does not confront is how such mobilization, integration, and change of government can take place.[29] He is clear on the "what kind" and "why" questions relating to government forms, but not on the "how."

Like Spengler, Robert E. Scott clearly uses a Western model. His article[30] attempts to show how Latin America could (and should) become more like his idealized portrayal of the United States. First, it should develop political specialists (this he would call "mobilization") rather than the amateur, part-time politicians who at the present time also serve as "functional" elites. He finds, probably correctly, that instability in the region is caused by factionalism among the competing elites. What Latin American countries need, he thinks, is consensus at the top, with each developing a stable power elite. The internal situation would then be considerably defused by the separation of political and technical functions.[31] He leaves unclear the means by which consensus could be established, and he ignores the *political* nature of Latin American (and, of course, past Western) development, given the region's world position.

The current dissension at the top puts much decision making in the hands of the President. Although Scott is fully aware that he is usually first a tool for special interests and then a scapegoat for policy failures, the potential for nation-building and economic initiative rests with him. But the masses, claims Scott, are too suspicious of change to throw their support to such a "modernizing" or nation-building political figure (possible evidence to the contrary, for example, support for Perón and Castro, is overlooked).

What is needed for modernization is a change in the attitudes of both elites and masses, a change which Scott admits cannot readily be achieved. He therefore puts his trust in the "innovators" of the Western experience, the middle class and professionals. They may indeed be the best hope for structural change. But their chances of success are poorer than Scott admits. First, they are sophisticated moderns linked directly to the world consumer market. It is doubtful therefore that they would voluntarily support the austerity that rapid capital accumulation and the downplay of consumerism demands. Their natural affiliation is with the forces of law and order, and the advocates of sectoral modernization. The radical intellectuals may indeed want to mobilize the masses, and for ideological reasons they may be prepared to sacrifice short-term individual benefits of a material or consumerist nature. But their urbanity makes them ill-equipped for the former task, and their sacrifices are usually made in jail or in exile, rather than in positions of developmental leadership.

Scott warns of the heavy losses that would be incurred by mass revolution. These are undoubtedly very real—the loss of life during the Mexican revolution, for example, can hardly be thought desirable. But the losses that Scott mentions are far from complete, and possible gains are ignored. In revolution, he claims, political structures are emasculated. But by his own admission, in Latin America they already are. Empirical evidence suggests that by *successful* revolution, as opposed to inconclusive strife, political structures are in fact strengthened (Mexico and Cuba), even if Scott doesn't like the end product. True, the economy can be harmed by the flight of skilled (including professional) labor—the very people that he favors for developmental change—but the possible long-term gains for development are discounted. In economic terms, the loss of productivity may be offset by decreased dependence on foreign consumer goods, if "bourgeois" standards are rejected by the urban masses in the post-revolutionary period. Mexico, Cuba, Bolivia, and the Dominican Republic are cited as countries in which revolution harmed economic development. The first presumably has recovered, and perhaps the price of revolution was worthwhile. The other three countries clearly suffered in the short run, but Scott fails to take foreign pressures and retaliation into account as factors inimical to economic recovery.

The lack of political machinery capable of generating economic growth still remains the primary obstacle to development in most of the underdeveloped world. Whether the middle classes can generate such leadership and set national economic growth in motion, as Scott hopes, remains in doubt. But in view of widespread consumerism it seems unlikely. The probability of successful mass revolution—given current internal and external conditions—is similarly not very high. Unfortunately the continuation of stagnation, international dependence, and domestic repression to maintain the consumerist sector is perhaps a more "stable" condition than optimists like Scott and myself would like to admit.

NOTES

1. Studies on the effects of the media in underdeveloped countries, and for that matter in developed countries too, are extremely rare. Field investigation of consumerism and producerism effects of the media would be a valuable supplement to the basically institutional argument presented here.
2. *The Rockefeller Report on the Americas* (Chicago: Quadrangle, 1969) did urge support for educational radio and TV in rural areas, but its specific communications recommendations were concerned only with U.S. image building in the region. See pp. 116, 137-140.
3. Skornia, *op. cit.,* p. 12.
4. S. I. Hayakawa, "Advertising versus Proper Evaluation: A review of *Reality in Advertising* by R. Reeves (New York: Knopf, 1961)," in *ETC. A Review of General Semantics,* vol. 18, no. 3, pp. 367-374, October, 1961, quoted in Skornia, *op. cit.,* p. 156.
5. The mass media could, of course, conceivably be used to help stem this population growth by spreading—and "selling"—information on birth control. There presumably are people available with sufficient skills in successful advertising approaches.
6. It could be argued with the corporations that this is totalitarian, and indeed the media have been used for effecting political control and indoctrination. Using controls to foster producerism may also be seen as forcing outside standards on the audience. This is not denied here. It is only argued that this imposition would be more in the interests of the masses than the present *direct* imposition of consumer styles by alien corporations. For a strong well-documented argument that U.S. domestic media are far from "value free," see Robert Cirino, *Don't Blame the People* (Los Angeles: Diversity Press, 1971).
7. This probably applies equally to other Western developed countries.
8. Most apologists for international corporate expansion stress the unifying benefits of such spread. The long-term outcome is assumed to be mutually beneficial. It is argued here that this may not necessarily be the case; that international operation weakens governmental controls on the corporation and "the general good" reverts to the more

narrow interests of the corporation. International regulatory powers which would define the "general good" on a global rather than national scale, despite efforts by the U.N., unfortunately do not exist at present.

9. Ideally this would be a United Nations responsibility, but since most of the financing would still have to come from the United States, it is more likely that the United States would prefer to dispense its resources—and receive the credit due—unilaterally.

10. UNESCO, *Twenty Years of Mass Communications in UNESCO,* GC/14/Press/7 (Mimeo), 2 pp.

11. UNESCO, *Twenty Years of UNESCO in Latin America,* CG/14/Press/10 (Mimeo), 3 pp.

12. See F. G. Burke, *Africa's Quest for Order* (Englewood Cliffs, N.J.: Prentice-Hall, 1964), pp. 37-44.

13. I. L. Horowitz, *Three Worlds of Development* (New York: Oxford University Press, 1966), p. 392. He makes much the same comment on Mexican and Brazilian cities, which exhibit the "style" but not the "substance" of modernization. See his article "The City as a Crucible for Political Action," in Glenn H. Beyer (ed.), *The Urban Explosion in Latin America* (Ithaca: Cornell University Press, 1967).

14. *Ibid.,* p. 400.

15. See, for example, Glaucio A. D. Soares, "Economic Development and Class Structure," in R. Bendix and S. M. Lipset (eds.), *Class, Status, and Power,* 2d ed. (New York: Free Press, 1966), pp. 190-199. According to the previously cited Rockefeller report (p. 119), the proportion of the economically active population in Latin America classified as "miscellaneous services" rose from 13% in 1950 to 15.6% in 1960, 16.6% in 1965, and 17.3% in 1969.

16. Solon T. Kimball, "Education and Developmental Change," in Art Gallaher, Jr. (ed.) *Perspectives in Developmental Change* (Lexington: University of Kentucky Press, 1968), pp. 71-100.

17. A. Anderson, in his article "Modernization of Education," argues for general primary expansion, while E. Shils, in "Modernization and Higher Education," stresses university development. Both articles appear in M. Weiner (ed.), *Modernization: The Dynamics of Growth* (New York: Basic Books, 1966).

18. To reduce costs in higher education, many less developed countries send their best students to the universities of developed countries for advanced training. This of course exposes them fully to consumerism. In addition, some remain in the developed country permanently—their talent and the educational investment in them are lost by their less developed native country. It has been calculated that the cost to the United States of educating students from less developed countries may be more than offset by the contributions of those who stay. See Harry G. Johnson, *Economic Policy Toward Less Developed Countries* (Washington, D.C.: Brookings Institution, 1967), p. 109.

19. S. H. Wellisz, "The Modernization of Technology," in Weiner, *op. cit.,* p. 233.

20. R. L. Meier, *Science and Economic Development,* 2d ed. (Cambridge, Mass.: MIT Press, 1966).

21. R. C. Wood, "The Future of Modernization," in Weiner, *op. cit.*

22. Wellisz, *loc. cit.*

23. U.N. Economic Commission for Africa, *Scientific Research in Africa* (Paris: UNESCO, 1966), p. 89.

24. This assumption has been denied by some economists who see tariff barriers as the major inhibitor of growth in the Third World. For this free trade view, see Johnson, *op. cit.,* especially pp. 98-99.

25. Rather than a flat contribution, it has been suggested that per family income be a basis for determining a developed nation's contribution to capital aid. Schedules based on a progressive tax principle can be calculated. For example, see P. N. Rosenstein-Rodan, "International Aid for Underdeveloped Countries," *Review of Economics and Statistics,* May, 1961, reprinted in M. F. Millikan and D. L. M. Blackmer (eds.), *The Emerging Nations: Their Growth and United States Policy* (Boston: Little, Brown and Company [for the Center for International Studies, MIT], 1961), pp. 158-169. Like the United Nations proposal, this has obviously not been accepted by the richer countries.

26. J. J. Spengler, "Economic Development: Political Preconditions and Political Consequences," in Finkle and Gable, *op. cit.,* pp. 253-268.
27. The norm among Western scholars is apparently to justify one party rule in underdeveloped countries. The rationale is that such regimes can bring about the discipline that rapid development requires. What is needed, according to Myrdal, are: "hard," not "soft," States. See G. Myrdal, *Asian Drama* (New York: Pantheon, 1968). For a dissenting view, see William McCord, *The Springtime of Freedom* (New York: Oxford University Press, 1965). S. Andreski also favors nonauthoritarian systems, since they are likely to be less corrupt. For Africa, he cites the Ivory Coast as a successful "free" government. See his *The African Predicament* (New York: Atherton, 1968). Unfortunately, such governments are also vulnerable to consumerism pressures from outside.
28. Ramon R. Gomez, "ECLA, Prebisch, and the Problem of Latin American Development," *Studies in Comparative International Development,* vol. II, no. 8, 1966. Raul Prebisch as an ECLA employee was the author of *Towards a New Policy for Development* (New York: United Nations, 1964).
29. Allende's electoral victory may indicate a peaceful method of governmental change. But to date it is by no means certain that his regime will survive, nor that it will be a developmental success.
30. Robert E. Scott, "Political Elites and Political Mobilization," in Lipset and Solari, *op. cit.,* pp. 117-145.
31. The clash between politicians and economic planners (*politicos* and *technicos*) in Mexico has been documented by Raymond Vernon, *The Dilemma of Mexico's Development* (Cambridge, Mass.: Harvard University Press, 1963). It illustrates that a specialization of functions does not automatically lead to harmony and consensus.

selected bibliography

I. GENERAL SOCIAL AND ECONOMIC DEVELOPMENT

A. Books and Articles

Adleman, Irma, and Cynthia T. Morris. *Society, Politics, and Economic Development.* Baltimore: Johns Hopkins Press, 1967.

Almond, G. A., and J. S. Coleman (eds.). *The Politics of Developing Areas.* Princeton, N.J.: Princeton University Press, 1960.

Andreski, Stanislav. *Parasitism and Subversion: The Case of Latin America.* New York: Pantheon, 1967.

_____. *The African Predicament.* New York: Atherton, 1968.

Appelbaum, Richard P. *Theories of Social Change.* Chicago: Markham, 1970.

Apter, David. *The Politics of Modernization.* Chicago: University of Chicago Press, 1965.

Aron, Raymond. *Main Currents in Sociological Thought.* Vol. 1. New York: Basic Books, 1965.

Ayres, C. E. *The Theory of Economic Progress,* 2d ed. New York: Schocken, 1962.

Baran, Paul A. *The Political Economy of Growth.* New York: Monthly Review Press, 1957.

Barnett, H. G., and Chandler Morse. *Scarcity and Growth.* Baltimore: Johns Hopkins University Press, 1963.

Barringer, H. R., G. I. Blanksten, and R. W. Mack (eds.). *Social Change in Developing Areas.* Boston: Schenkman, 1965.

Bendix, Reinhard. *Nation-Building and Citizenship.* New York: John Wiley & Sons, 1964.

_____, and S. M. Lipset (eds.). *Class, Status and Power,* 2d ed. New York: Free Press, 1966.

Beyer, Glenn H. (ed.). *The Urban Explosion in Latin America.* Ithaca: Cornell University Press, 1967.

Black, Cyril E. *The Dynamics of Modernization.* New York: Harper and Row, 1966.

Blumer, Herbert. "The Idea of Social Development." *Studies in Comparative International Development.* Vol. II, no. 1, 1966.

Braibanti, Ralph J., and J. J. Spengler (eds.). *Administration and Economic Development in India.* Durham, N.C.: Duke University Press for Duke University Commonwealth Studies Center, 1963.

────. *Tradition, Values, and Socio-economic Development.* Durham, N.C.: Duke University Press for Duke University Commonwealth Studies Center, 1961.

Burke, Fred G. *Africa's Quest for Order.* Englewood Cliffs, N.J.: Prentice-Hall, 1964.

Business International. *The United Nations and the Business World.* (Research Report #57-4). New York: Business International, 1967.

Chandresekhar, S. (ed.). *Asia's Population Problems.* New York: Praeger, 1967.

Chenery, H. B., and M. Bruno. "Development Alternatives in an Open Economy." *Economic Journal,* March, 1962, pp. 79-103.

Cleveland, Harlan (ed.). *The Promise of World Tensions.* New York: Macmillan, 1961.

Cochrane, Alynn. *Development Anthropology.* New York: Oxford University Press, 1971.

Coleman, James Smoot (ed.). *Education and Political Development.* Princeton, N.J.: Princeton University Press, 1965.

Dumont, René, *False Start in Africa,* 2 ed., rev., trans. by Phyllis Nauts Ott. New York: Praeger, 1969.

Durkheim, Emile. *The Division of Labor in Society,* trans. by George Simpson. New York: Free Press paperback edition, 1964.

Eisenstadt, S. N. *Modernization: Protest and Change.* Englewood Cliffs, N.J.: Prentice-Hall, 1966.

────. *The Political Systems of Empires.* Glencoe, Ill.: Free Press, 1963.

────. "Problems of Integration and Modernization Breakdowns." *Economic Development and Cultural Change,* 12, July, 1964, pp. 345-367.

────(ed.). *Readings in Social Evolution and Development.* New York: Pergamon, 1970.

Expert Working Group on Social Aspects of Economic Development in Latin America. *Social Aspects of Economic Development in*

Latin America. Vol. 1, Egbert de Vries and Jose Medina Echavarria (eds.). Paris: UNESCO (official sponsor), 1963.

Fanon, Frantz. *The Wretched of the Earth,* trans. by Constance Farrington. New York: Grove Press, Evergreen Black Cat Edition, 1968.

Felix, David. "Monetarists, Structuralists, and Import Substituting Industrialization: A Critical Appraisal." *Studies in Comparative International Development.* Vol. I, no. 10, 1965.

————. "Latin America: Take-offs into Unsustained Growth." *Social Research,* August, 1969.

Field, Arthur J. (ed.). *City and Country in the Third World.* Cambridge, Mass.: Schenkman, 1970.

Finkle, J. L., and R. W. Gable (eds.). *Political Development and Social Change.* New York: John Wiley & Sons, 1966.

Furtado, Celso. *Development and Underdevelopment.* Berkeley and Los Angeles: University of California Press, 1967.

Galbraith, J. K. *Economic Development.* Cambridge, Mass.: Harvard University Press, 1966.

Gallaher, Art, Jr. (ed.). *Perspectives in Developmental Change.* Lexington: University of Kentucky Press, 1968.

Geiger, Theodore. *The Conflicted Relationship.* New York: McGraw-Hill (for the Council on Foreign Relations), 1967.

Germani, Gino. "Social Change and Intergroup Conflicts," in *The New Sociology,* ed. by Irving L. Horowitz. New York: Oxford University Press, 1964.

————. "Mass Immigration and Modernization in Argentina." *Studies in Comparative International Development.* Vol. II, no. 11, 1966.

Gerschenkron, A. *Economic Backwardness in Historical Perspective.* Cambridge, Mass.: Belknap Press of Harvard University Press, 1962.

Gomez, Ramon R. "ECLA, Prebisch and the Problem of Latin American Development." *Studies in Comparative International Development:* Vol. II, no. 8, 1966.

Halmos, P. (ed.). *The Development of Industrial Societies.* Keele: *Sociological Review* Monograph, no. 8, October, 1964.

Hirschman, Albert O. *Development Projects Observed.* Washington, D.C.: The Brookings Institution, 1967.

Hobsbawm, E. J. *Industry and Empire.* New York: Pantheon, 1968.

Horowitz, Irving L. *Three Worlds of Development.* New York: Oxford University Press, 1966.

_____. "The Norm of Illegitimacy." *Soundings.* Vol. II, no. 1, Spring, 1968.

Hoselitz, B. F. *The Progress of Underdeveloped Areas.* Chicago: University of Chicago Press, 1952.

Jaffe, A. J. *People, Jobs and Economic Development.* New York: Free Press, 1959.

Janowitz, Morris. *The Military in the Political Development of New Nations.* Chicago: University of Chicago Press, 1964.

Johnson, Harry G. *Economic Policies Toward Less Developed Countries.* Washington, D.C.: The Brookings Institution, 1967.

Kassalow, E. M. (ed.). *The Role of Social Security in Economic Development.* U.S. Department of Health, Education, and Welfare: Social Security Administration, Office of Research and Statistics, Research Report No. 27. Washington, D.C.: U.S. Government Printing Office, 1968.

Kunkel, John H. *Society and Economic Growth.* New York: Oxford University Press, 1970.

Kuznets, A. S. *Modern Economic Growth.* New Haven: Yale University Press, 1966.

Levy, Marion. *Modernization and the Structure of Societies.* Vol. I. Princeton: Princeton University Press, 1966.

Lipset, S. M., and A. Solari (eds.). *Elites in Latin America.* New York: Oxford University Press, 1967.

Magnin, William (ed.). *Peasants in Cities.* Boston: Houghton Mifflin, 1970.

Marsh, R. M. *Comparative Sociology.* New York: Harcourt, Brace & World, 1967.

McCord, William. *The Springtime of Freedom.* New York: Oxford University Press, 1965.

McLeish, John. *The Theory of Social Change.* New York: Schocken Books, 1969

Meadows, Paul, and Ephraim H. Mizruchi (eds.). *Urbanism, Urbanization, and Change: Comparative Perspectives.* Reading, Mass.: Addison-Wesley, 1969.

Merhav, Meir. *Technological Dependence, Monopoly and Growth.* New York: Pergamon, 1969.

Millikan, M. F., and D. L. M. Blackmer (eds.). *The Emerging Nations: Their Growth and United States Policy.* Boston: Little, Brown and Company (for Center for International Studies, MIT), 1961.

Mills, C. Wright. *Power, Politics and People,* ed. by I. L. Horowitz. New York: Ballantine, 1963.

Moore, W. E. *Impact of Industry.* Englewood Cliffs, N.J.: Prentice-Hall, 1965.

————, and A. S. Feldman (eds.). *Labor Commitment and Social Change in Developing Areas.* New York: Social Science Council, 1960.

Myrdal, Gunnar. *Asian Drama: An Inquiry into the Poverty of Nations.* New York: Pantheon, 1968, 3 vols.

Nash, Manning. *Primitive and Peasant Economic Systems.* San Francisco: Chandler, 1966.

Ness, Gayl D. (ed.). *The Sociology of Economic Development.* New York: Harper and Row, 1970.

Nettl, J. P., and Roland Robertson. *International Systems and the Modernization of Societies.* New York: Basic Books, 1968.

Nisbet, Robert A. *Social Change and History.* New York: Oxford University Press, 1969.

Olivos, Luis. *Population Policies and Development in the Year 2000.* Washington, D.C.: Pan American Union, General Secretariat of the OAS, Dept. of Social Affairs, UP/Ser.H/VII.69, January, 1969.

Papanek, G. F. (ed.)., *Development Policy—Theory and Practice.* Cambridge, Mass.: Harvard University Press, 1968.

Pearson, Lester B. (Chairman). *Partners in Development: Report of the Commission on International Development.* New York: Praeger, 1969.

Petras, James. *Politics and Social Forces in Chilean Development.* Berkeley and Los Angeles: University of California Press, 1969.

Redfield, Robert. *The Folk Culture of Yucatan.* Chicago: University of Chicago Press, 1941.

Rockefeller, Nelson A. *The Rockefeller Report on the Americas.* Chicago: Quadrangle, 1969.

Rostow, Walt W. *The Stages of Economic Growth.* New York: Cambridge University Press, 1960.

Spengler, J. J., and O. D. Duncan (eds.). *Population Theory and Policy.* Glencoe, Ill.: Free Press, 1956.

Stanley, Manfred. "Social Development as a Normative Concept." *Journal of Developing Areas,* I, April, 1967, pp. 301-316.

Streeten, Paul. "Critique of Development Concepts." *European Journal of Sociology,* vol. XI, no. 1, pp. 67-80.

Tonnies, Ferdinand. *Community and Society,* trans. by Charles P. Loomis. New York: Harper Torchbook, 1963.

Tumin, Melvin. *Social Class and Social Change in Puerto Rico.* Princeton: Princeton University Press, 1961.

United Nations Economic Commission for Latin America. *The Process of Industrial Development in Latin America.* New York: United Nations, 1966.

Veblen, T. *The Theory of the Leisure Class.* New York: Mentor, 1953.

Vernon, Raymond. *The Dilemma of Mexico's Development; The Roles of Private and Public Sectors.* Cambridge, Mass.: Harvard University Press, 1963.

_____. *Public Policy and Private Enterprise in Mexico.* Cambridge, Mass.: Harvard University Press, 1964.

Wallerstein, Immanual (ed.). *Social Change: The Colonial Situation.* New York: Wiley, 1966.

Ward, Barbara. *The Rich Nations and the Poor Nations.* New York: W. W. Norton, 1963.

Weiner, Myron (ed.). *Modernization: The Dynamics of Growth.* New York: Basic Books, 1966.

Whyte, William F., and Lawrence K. Williams. *Toward an Integrated Theory of Development.* Ithaca: New York State School of Industrial and Labor Relations, Cornell University, I.L.R. Paperback No. 5, 1968.

B. Journals and Periodicals

Comparative Political Studies, Sage Publications (Quarterly).

Comparative Studies in Society and History, Cambridge University Press (Quarterly).

Economic Developments and Cultural Change (1952-), University of Chicago Periodicals.

International Development Review (Quarterly).

International Journal, Toronto.

International Journal of Comparative Sociology.

International Social Science Journal, UNESCO (Quarterly).
Journal of Developing Areas.
Journal of Development Studies (1964-), London.
Studies in Comparative International Development, Sage Publications (occasional papers).

C. Bibliographies, Yearbooks, etc.

Agency for International Development. *Latin America: Economic Growth Trends*, Office of Program and Policy Coordination, Statistics Reports Division, December, 1968.

————. *Gross National Product: Growth Rates and Trend Data*, Office of Program and Policy Coordination, Statistics and Reports Division, RC-W-138, April 25, 1969.

————. *Summary Economic and Social Indicators 18 Latin American Countries: 1960-1970.* Office of Development Programs, Bureau for Latin America, April, 1971.

Alexander-Frutschi, Marian Crites (ed.). *Human Resources and Economic Growth*, Menlo Park, Calif.: Stanford Research Institute, 1963.

Banks, A. S., and R. B. Textor. *A Cross-Policy Survey.* Cambridge, Mass.: MIT Press, 1963.

Baranson, Jack. *Technology for Underdeveloped Areas.* London: Pergamon Press, 1967.

Russett, Bruce M. *World Handbook of Political and Social Indicators.* New Haven: Yale University Press, 1964.

Social Progress Trust Fund, Seventh through Tenth Annual Reports, 1967-1970, *Socio-Economic Progress in Latin America.* Washington, D.C.: Inter-American Development Bank, 1968-1971.

United Nations Economic Commission for Latin America, *Statistical Bulletin for Latin America*, vol. III, no. 1. New York: United Nations, 1966.

United Nations, *U.N. Demographic Yearbook, 1967; U.N. Statistical Yearbook, 1967, 1968, 1969; Yearbook of International Trade Statistics, 1966; Yearbook of National Accounts Statistics, 1966.*

United Nations, Department of Economic and Social Affairs, *The External Financing of Economic Development.* New York: United Nations, 1970.

II. INDIVIDUAL AND PSYCHOLOGICAL ASPECTS OF DEVELOPMENT

Books and Articles

Barnett, H. G. *Innovation: The Basis of Cultural Change.* New York: McGraw-Hill, 1953.

Bourricaud, François. "Structure and Function of the Peruvian Oligarchy." *Studies in Comparative International Development,* vol. 11, no. 2, 1966.

Bradburn, N. N., and D. E. Berlew. "Need for Achievement and English Industrial Growth." *Economic Development and Cultural Change,* vol. 10, no. 1, October, 1961, pp. 8-21.

Cardoso, Fernando H. "The Entrepreneurial Elites of Latin America." *Studies in Comparative International Development,* vol. 11, no. 10, 1966.

Doob, Leonard W. "Scales for Assaying Psychological Modernization in Africa." *The Public Opinion Quarterly,* 1967, XXXI(*3*), pp. 414-421.

Eisenstadt, S. N. (ed.). *The Protestant Ethic and Modernization.* New York: Basic Books, 1968.

Frank, Andrew G. "Urban Poverty in Latin America." *Studies in Comparative International Development,* vol. 11, no. 5, 1966.

Hagen, Everett E. *On the Theory of Social Change.* Homewood, Ill.: Dorsey, 1962.

Kahl, J. A. *The Measurement of Modernism.* Austin: University of Texas Press, 1968.

Inkeles, Alex. "Industrial Man." *American Journal of Sociology,* LXVI, July, 1960, pp. 1-31.

LeVine, R. A. *Dreams and Deeds.* Chicago: University of Chicago Press, 1966.

McClelland, David C. *The Achieving Society.* Princeton: Van Nostrand, 1961.

――――, and David G. Winter. *Motivating Economic Achievement.* New York: Free Press, 1969.

Schnaiberg, Allan. "Measuring Modernism: Theoretical and Empirical Explorations." *American Journal of Sociology,* vol. 76, no. 3, November, 1970, pp. 399-425.

Smith, D. H., and Alex Inkeles. "The O. M. Scale: A Comparative

Socio-Psychological Measure of Individual Modernity." *Sociometry*, 29, December, 1966, pp. 353-377.
Weber, Max. *The Protestant Ethic and the Spirit of Capitalism*, Trans. by Talcott Parsons. New York: Charles Scribner's Sons, 1958.

III. COMMUNICATIONS AND THE DEVELOPMENTAL EFFECTS OF MASS MEDIA

A. Books and Articles
Barnouw, Erik. *The Image Empire.* New York: Oxford University Press, 1970.
Barrett, Marvin (ed.). *Survey of Broadcast Journalism, 1968-1969* and *1969-70.* New York: Grosset and Dunlap, 1969 and 1970.
Browne, Don R. "The American Image as Presented Abroad by U.S. Television." *Journalism Quarterly,* Summer, 1966, pp. 307-316.
Cirino, Robert. *Don't Blame the People.* Los Angeles: University Press, 1971.
De Fleur, Melvin L. *Theories of Mass Communication.* New York: McKay, 1966.
Deutsch, Karl W. "Social Mobilization and Political Development." *American Political Science Review,* 55, pp. 493-514.
Deutschman, P. J., H. Ellingsworth, and J. T. McNelly. *Communications and Social Change in Latin America.* New York: Praeger, 1968.
Dizard, W. *Television: A World View.* Syracuse: Syracuse University Press, 1966.
Edelstein, Alex S. *Perspectives in Mass Communications.* Copenhagen: Einar Harcks Forlag, 1966.
Educational Policies Commission. *Mass Communication and Education.* Washington, D.C.: National Education Association of the United States, 1968.
Ellul, Jacques. *Propaganda,* trans. by Konrad Kellen and Jean Lerner. New York: Knopf, 1966.
Estrada, Luis P., and Daniel Hopen. *The Cultural Value of Film and Television in Latin America.* (Translated from the Spanish). Paris: UNESCO (limited distribution, mimeo), SHC/CS/158/4, July 9, 1968.

Frappier, J. "U.S. Media Empire/Latin America." *NACLA Newsletter,* New York: North American Congress on Latin America, vol. 11, no. 9, January, 1969, pp. 1-11.

Johnson, Nicholas. *How to Talk Back to Your Television Set.* Boston: Atlantic-Little, Brown and Company, 1970.

Katz, Elihu, and Paul Lazarsfeld. *Personal Influence.* Glencoe, Ill.: Free Press, 1955.

Klapper, Joseph T. *The Effects of Mass Communications.* Glencoe, Ill.: Free Press, 1960.

Lerner, Daniel, and W. Schramm (eds.). *Communications and Change in the Developing Countries.* Honolulu: East-West Center Press, 1967.

Lerner, Daniel. "Toward a Communication Theory of Modernization," in L. Pye (ed.), *Communications and Political Development.* Princeton: Princeton University Press, 1963.

——————. *The Passing of Traditional Society.* New York: Free Press, 1958.

——————. "Communications Systems and Social Systems," in W. Schramm (ed.), *Mass Communications.* Urbana: University of Illinois Press, 1961.

McGinniss, Joe. *The Selling of the President 1968.* New York: Trident, 1969.

McLuhan, H. Marshall. *The Mechanical Bride: Folklore of Industrial Man.* New York: The Vanguard Press, 1951.

——————. *The Gutenberg Galaxy: The Making of Typographic Man.* Toronto: University of Toronto Press, 1962.

——————. *Understanding Media: The Extension of Man.* New York: McGraw-Hill, 1964.

——————. *The Medium is the Message* (with Quentin Fiore). New York: Random House, 1967.

McMillan, C., R. F. Gonzales, and L. G. Erickson. *International Enterprise in a Developing Economy.* Michigan State University, Bureau of Business and Economic Research, 1964.

Minor, Dale. *The Information War.* New York: Hawthorn Books, 1970.

Pool, Ithiel de Sola. "The Mass Media and Politics in the Modernization Process," in Lucian Pye, ed. *Communications and Political Development.*

_____. "Communications and Development," in M. Weiner (ed.), *Modernization: The Dynamics of Growth.* New York: Basic Books, 1966.

Pye, Lucian B. (ed.). *Communications and Political Development.* Princeton: Princeton University Press, 1963.

Qualter, Terence H. *Propaganda and Psychological Warfare.* New York: Random House, 1962.

Schramm, Wilbur (ed.). *Mass Communications.* Urbana: University of Illinois Press, 1960.

_____. *Mass Media and National Development.* Stanford, Calif: Stanford University Press, 1964.

Schiller, Herbert I. *Mass Communications and American Empire.* New York: Augustus M. Kelley, 1969.

Simmons, Robert E., Kurt Kent, and Vishiva M. Mishra. "Media and Development News in the Slums of Ecuador and India." *Journalism Quarterly,* Winter, 1968, pp. 698-705.

Skornia, H. J. *Television and Society.* New York: McGraw-Hill, 1965.

Stearn, G. E. (ed.). *McLuhan: Hot and Cool.* New York: Dial Press, 1967.

Stevenson, William. *The Play Theory of Mass Communication.* Chicago: University of Chicago Press, 1967.

U.S. AID. *Education Television Project—Colombia.* Staff report, mimeo, undated.

UNESCO. *Mass Media in the Developing Countries.* Paris: UNESCO, 1961.

Wells, Alan. "Communications and Development: The Relevance of Media Content." *The Sociological Quarterly,* 12, Winter, 1971, pp. 95-99.

B. Periodicals and Trade Journals

Advertising Age (Trade).

Broadcasting (Trade).

CETO Review, Quarterly, Center for Educational TV Overseas, London.

Columbia Journal Review.

European Broadcasting Union Review, Geneva (Bi-monthly).

International Radio and TV Organization, Prague (Bi-monthly).

Journal of Broadcasting, University of California.

Journalism Quarterly.
Marketing/Communications (formerly *Printers' Ink*).
Public Opinion Quarterly.
Telecasting.
Telefilm International, Los Angeles.
Television and Adult Education, Paris.
Television Age (especially semi-annual issues featuring overseas development).
Television Digest.
Television Magazine (Trade).
Television Quarterly, Syracuse University.
Variety.

C. Yearbooks and Data Compendiums

ABC International Television, Inc. *Worldvision, Your Passport to the Future.*
ABC. *Television in the Space Age,* Proceedings of the first Worldvision Symposium held in Washington, D.C. under the auspices of ABC International, March 21, 1965.
Broadcasting Yearbook.
Federal Communications Commission. *The FCC in Fiscal 1968—A Summary of Activities.* Washington, D.C.: FCC, 1968.
International Advertising Association. *Advertising Investments Around the World—The Five Year Trend.* New York: IAA, October, 1965.
———. *Advertising Investments Around the World* (Eighth Biennial Report). New York: IAA, December, 1967.
———. *World Advertising Expenditures* (Ninth IAA Biennial Survey conducted by International Research Associates). New York: IAA, 1970.
International T.V. Almanac, Aaronson, C. S. (ed.), New York: Quigley Publications, 1968, 1969, 1970 editions.
Standard Directory of Advertising Agencies. National Register Publishing Co., Inc., Skokie, Ill.: June, 1968, no. 157.
Television Factbook, 1967.
UNESCO. *World Radio & Television.* Paris: UNESCO, 1965.
———. *Statistical Yearbook.*
———. *Basic Facts and Figures.*

_____. International Institute for Educational Planning. *The New Media,* Paris: 1967.

U.S. Information Agency, Research and Reference Service. *Overseas Television Growth in 1965,* R-111-66, June, 1966. *Overseas Television Developments in 1964,* R-51-65, April, 1965, and *1963,* R-45-64, April, 1964.

USIA. *30th* and *31st Review of Operations,* Jan.-June, July-Dec., 1968.

_____. (Management Division). *The Agency in Brief, 1969.*

World Radio—TV Handbook, 18th ed., O. Lund Johansen (ed.). Hellerup, Denmark: 1964.

Tables

TABLE I

GROWTH RATES BY ECONOMIC LEVEL, 51 NON-COMMUNIST COUNTRIES

Growth Rate (Annual G.D.P. Growth, 1960-1966)

Economic level (1963, G.N.P. per capita U.S. dollars)	5% or more	Less than 5%
600 or more	11	11
Less than 600	17	12

Source: Diagram 2, *UN Statistical Yearbook, 1967.*

TABLE II

GROWTH RATES BY ECONOMIC LEVEL, 110 COUNTRIES

Growth Rate

Level (G.N.P. per capita)	High	Low
Very high, medium	13	28
Very low and low	49	20

n = 110

Source: A. S. Banks and R. B. Textor, *A Cross Polity Survey* (Cambridge, Mass.: MIT Press, 1963), 28/36 Matrix.

TABLE III

CORRELATION MATRIX OF MEDIA USE
AND FOUR SOCIAL VARIABLES[a]

	Per capita income	Literacy	Urbanization (% in localities over 2000)	% Employed in non-agriculture
Newsprint consumption per capita	.83	.82	.69	.68
Newspaper circulation per 100 persons	.83	.79	.75	.51
Cinema seating capacity per 100 persons	.80	.68	.86	.82
Radio receivers per 100 persons	.86	.72	.71	.78
Television receivers per 100 persons[b]	.83	.60	.80	.92

[a]All underdeveloped countries of Asia, Africa, and Latin America with populations greater than one half million persons reporting for the 1957-1959 period.
[b]Latin America only.
Source: UNESCO, *Mass Media in the Developing Countries* (Paris: UNESCO, 1961), p. 17.

TABLE IV

MEDIA DISTRIBUTION IN MAJOR
UNDERDEVELOPED REGIONS, APPROXIMATELY 1960

	United Nations Standard	South East Asia (27 countries, excluding Japan)	Latin America (34 states, South and Central America)	Africa (all countries)	Middle East (13 countries excluding Israel)
Daily newspaper circulation per 100 persons	10	1.4	7.4	1.2	1.4
Radio receivers per 100 persons	5	0.7	9.8	1.8	2.2
Cinema seats per 100 persons	2	0.7	3.5	0.5	0.6

Source: Compiled from UNESCO, *Mass Media in the Developing Countries* (Paris: UNESCO, 1961), pp. 18-33.

TABLE V

SOUTH ASIAN MEDIA AND GNP PER CAPITA, SELECTED COUNTRIES

	Per capita GNP, '63 US $	Circulation of daily newspapers per 100 inhabitants (UN standard: 10)[a]			Radio receivers per 100 inhabitants (UN standard: 5)[b]			Television receivers per 100 people (UN standard: 2)[c]	
		1952	1960	1968	1950	1960	1968	1965	1968
	(1)	(2)	(3)	(4)	(5)	(6)	(7)	(8)	(9)
Malaya	275	5.0[d]	3.4	7.4	1.0	3.6	4.8	1.1	1.4
Philippines	251	1.9	1.8	2.7	0.4	2.2	1.8	0.3	0.5
Ceylon	145	2.9	3.7	4.4	0.4	3.6	3.3	—	—
Thailand	115	0.4	1.4	2.2	0.5	0.7	8.2	0.6	.62
Indonesia	95	0.7	1.1	0.7	0.3	0.7	1.3	0.04	0.06
Pakistan	93	0.2	0.7	1.8	0.1	0.3	1.05	0.002	0.03
India	92	0.7	1.1	1.3	0.1	0.5	1.8	—	0.0015
Burma	72	0.8	1.2	0.9	0.1	0.6	1.5	—	—

[a] Figures for Indonesia and Pakistan are for 1965; Philippines, Thailand, and Burma for 1966.

[b] Philippine figure is for 1966; Thailand, Indonesia, and Pakistan for 1967.

[c] Philippine figure is for 1967.

[d] Figure includes Singapore.

Source: Column 1 — *UN Statistical Yearbook, 1968.*
Columns 2, 3, 5, 6 — Adapted from G. Myrdal, *Asian Drama* (New York: Pantheon, 1968), p. 1,693—compiled from various U.N. sources—a minority of the figures refer to the year before or after that of the column heading.
Column 4 — *U.N. Statistical Yearbook*, 1969, pp. 748-749.
Columns 7, 9 — Computed from receiver statistics (pp. 756, 758) and 1968 population estimates (p. 61), *U.N. Statistical Yearbook, 1969.*
Column 8 — Compiled from United States Information Agency data for receivers and U.N. estimates of population for 1966, *UN Statistical Yearbook, 1968.*

TABLE VI

GROWTH OF OVERSEAS TELEVISION IN
UNDERDEVELOPED AREAS, 1955-1965

TV Sets in use (rounded thousands)

End of year	Near East and South Asia	Africa	Far East	Latin American and Caribbean
1955	0	5	260	619
1956	0	5	488	1,190
1957	4	11	1,124	1,561
1958	11	25	2,530	2,314
1959	46	44	5,118	2,525
1960	151	69	7,946	3,554
1961	306	96	10,241	4,552
1962	408	128	14,797	5,183
1963	725	250	18,895	6,143
1964	939	277	20,977	6,645
1965	1,039	313	23,842	7,548
1968*	1,325	846	22,077	9,708

*Computed from individual country listings in *U.N. Statistical Yearbook, 1969*, p. 758. Some countries did not report, but with the exception of the Far East even these partial totals show a continuation of television expansion.

Source: Adapted from United States Information Agency (Research and Reference Service), *Overseas Television Growth in 1965*, R-111-66, June, 1966, p. 4. This was the last in a series of reports on overseas television conducted by the Agency.

TABLE VII

ECONOMIC LEVEL, LITERACY, AND MEDIA AVAILABILITY, 17 LATIN AMERICAN COUNTRIES IN THE SIXTIES

	Gross national product/capita 1963 (U.S. dollars) (1)	Per cent adult literacy (2)	Newspaper circulation per 1000 inhabitants (3)	Cinema seating per 1000 inhabitants (4)	Radio receivers per 100 inhabitants (5)
Venezuela	768	76.2	70	—	19.4
Argentina	566	91.4	148	—	16.7
Uruguay	525	90.3	314	71	35.4
Panama	466	76.7	78	49	17.0
Mexico	386	65.4	116	34	10.0
Costa Rica	384	84.4	77	63	6.9
Chile	327	83.6	118	31	13.8
Colombia	309	72.9	52	26	15.3
Nicaragua	303	49.8	49	—	6.8
Brazil	300	61.0	33	26	6.6
Dominican Rep.	288	64.5	27	14	5.0
Guatemala	287	37.9	31	18	5.6
El Salvador	249	49.0	47	21	13.4
Peru	236	61.1	47	30	10.1
Honduras	203	45.0	19	22	6.4
Ecuador	186	67.5	45	23	4.1
Haiti	79	10.5	5	3	0.6

Sources: Column 1 — *United Nations Statistical Yearbook, 1968.*
  Column 2 — Social Progress Trust Fund, Seventh Annual Report, 1967, *Socio-Economic Progress in Latin America* (Washington, D.C.: Inter-American Development Bank, 1968). Year varies from 1960 to 1964. The figure for Haiti is for 1950.
  Columns 3 and 4 — *U.N. Statistical Yearbook, 1967*, pp. 763, 764; pp. 767-769. Figures are for various years between 1960 and 1965.
  Column 5 — UNESCO, *World Radio & Television*, pp. 59-67, pp. 75-83. Year varies between 1960 and 1962.

TABLE VIII

CORRELATION MATRIX: PER CAPITA GNP, LITERACY, AND THE MASS MEDIA

	Literacy	Newspapers	Cinema	Radio	Television
GNP/Capita	.79	.85	.80	.81	.89
Literacy	—	.89	.80	.70	.77
Newspapers	—	—	.86	.83	.78
Cinema	—	—	—	.70	.85
Radio	—	—	—	—	.79

Source: Correlations (Spearman's Rho) computed from data presented in Table VII and Column 6, Table IX.

176

TABLE IX

TELEVISION TRANSMITTING STATIONS AND RECEIVERS, SELECTED LATIN AMERICAN COUNTRIES[a] ORDERED BY GNP PER CAPITA[b]

	Transmitting stations			Receivers in use (thousands)		
	Programming 1964 (1)	Total 1964 (2)	Total 1967 (3)	Dec. 1964 (4)	1967 (5)	Receivers per 1000 people, 1967 (6)
Venezuela	6	21	21	401	650	73
Argentina	11	14	14	1,360	3,200	141
Uruguay	4	4	4	174	200	73
Panama	3	9	9	100	110	86
Mexico	24	32	43	1,071	2,100	48
Costa Rica	2	6	6	30	65	44
Chile	3	3	22	33	300	34
Colombia	2	14	14	350	410	22
Nicaragua	1	2	4	6	19	11
Brazil	33	42	42	2,156	5,000	60
Dominican Rep.	2	4	4	50	52	14
Guatemala	2	2	4	45	45	9.8
El Salvador	2	3	3	27	35	11.8
Peru	16	22	22	210	300	25
Honduras	1	3	5	8	15	6.3
Ecuador	3	3	6	40	45	8.5
Haiti	1	1	1	5	10	2.2

[a]Excludes television activities in the British Caribbean, Colonial Territories, and Cuba. Paraguay and Bolivia had no television.

[b]GNP/capita ranking is on the basis of 1963 data shown in Table VII.

Sources: Columns 1, 2, 4: U.S. Information Agency (Research Reference Service), *Overseas Television Developments in 1964*, R-51-65 (April, 1965), p. 51.
 Columns 3, 5: Frappier, *op. cit.*, p. 5, from USIA and *Television Age*, January, 1968.
 Column 6: Calculated from Column 6 and U.N. population estimates for 1966 (*U.N. Statistical Yearbook, 1968*).

TABLE X

GROWTH OF TELEVISION AND ECONOMIC GROWTH, 17 LATIN AMERICAN COUNTRIES, 1955-1960 AND 1960-1965

	(1) % Growth in receivers 1955-1960	(2) % Annual growth in GNP per capita 1955-1960	(3) % Growth in receivers 1960-1965[a]	(4) % Growth in GNP per capita 1960-1965[a]
Group I				
Countries				
Venezuela	570	3.6	195	6.9
Argentina	220	1.4	275	10.5
Mexico	500	2.6	115	17.9
Brazil	550	2.9	170	5.7
Colombia	766	0.7	100	7.8
Dominican Rep.	220	1.9	120	−10.9
Group II				
Countries				
Panama			710	26.8
Uruguay			1000	−3.6
Nicaragua			66	29.7
Peru			520	18.4
Guatemala			150	9.3
El Salvador			87	15.3
Group III				
Countries				
Chile			1275	10.7
Costa Rica			440	9.3
Ecuador			1000	6.1
Honduras			122	7.3
Haiti			300	−

[a] Data for Group III countries are for 1962-1966.

Sources: Columns 1 and 3: Calculated from receiver estimates, *U.N. Statistical Yearbook,* various editions, 1956-1968.

Column 2: Table 16, AID, *Gross National Product: Growth Rates and Trend Data,* April, 1969.

Column 3: Calculated from Table 3a, per capita GNP at constant 1967 prices, in *Ibid.*

178

TABLE XI

USIA STAFF AND FINANCES, 1965-1970

Fiscal year	Total positions	Total appropriations (thousands of dollars)
1965	12,028	165,854
1966	11,918	185,226
1967	12,106	172,748
1968	11,908	194,255
1969	10,984	177,535
1970 (estimated)	10,933	179,300

Source: USIA, *The Agency in Brief, 1969,* from two tables, p. 22.

TABLE XII

UNITED STATES INTEREST IN
LATIN AMERICAN PROGRAMMING STATIONS

Large countries*	Number of programming stations, 1964	Number in which there is known U.S. involvement		Small countries*	Programming stations, 1964	U.S. involvement
Brazil	33	2	Panama	3	2
Argentina	11	2	Costa Rica	2	1
Mexico	24	5	Dom. Rep.	2	1
Venezuela	6	5	Guatemala	2	1
Colombia	2	1	Ecuador	3	3
Chile	3	2	El Salvador	2	2
Peru	16	2	Nicaragua	1	1
Uruguay	4	1	Honduras	1	1
			Haiti	1	1

*Countries are listed in order of the number of television sets in use: Panama has less than Uruguay.

Sources: Total programming stations operating in 1964 from Table 9. U.S. involvement was computed from station listings in Frappier, *op. cit.*, and other fragmentary sources.

179

TABLE XIII

AVERAGE MONTHLY* U.S. TELEVISION RECEIVER
PRODUCTION AND DISTRIBUTOR SALES

(Number of sets in rounded thousands)

	Year	Monochrome	Color	Total
Production	1964	617	99	716
	1965	632	174	806
	1967	425	481	907
	1968	463	486	948
Distributor sales	1966	561	311	872
	1967	408	341	749
	1968	417	390	807
	1969	386	420	807

*Monthly averages for production in 1964 and 1965 have been calculated from the first seven months of each year, in 1967 and 1968 for all twelve months. Distributor sales averages were computed from totals for the first eight months of each year except for the 1969 averages, which are based on seven-month figures.

Source: Computed from Electronic Industries Association data, compiled and tabulated in C. S. Aaronson (ed.), *International T.V. Almanac* (New York: Quigley Publications, 1968-69-70 editions), pp. 22A, 24A.

TABLE XIV

ESTIMATED TV ADVERTISING EXPENDITURES
IN THE U.S. BY PRODUCT, 1966 AND 1968

(Rounded millions of dollars)

	1966	1968
Food, Drink, etc.	1279 (49.2%)	1309 (46.4%)
Ale, beer & wine	101	85
Confections, soft drinks	166	138
Drug products	243	259
Food & grocery	516	573
Pet products	40	47
Tobacco & supplies	213	208
Cleaning: Personal & Household	687 (26.4%)	880 (31.2%)
Cosmetics, toiletries	295	400
Dental products	112	104
Household cleaners, etc.	90	100
Laundry products	147	249
Household paper products	42	28
All Other Products	635 (24.4%)	634 (22.5%)
Automotive	160	199
Gasoline & lubricants	67	85
Total	2601 (100%)	2824 (100.1%)

Source: Expenditure by product from *International T.V. Almanac* (C. S. Aaronson, ed.) (New York: Quigley Publications, 1970), pp. 24A, 26A.

TABLE XV

ADVERTISING EXPENDITURES BY MEDIA, THE UNITED STATES AND SIX LATIN AMERICAN COUNTRIES, 1966 AND 1968

(In millions of U.S. dollars)

	Print		Radio		Television	
	1966	1968 (% Change)	1966	1968 (% Change)	1966	1968 (% Change)
United States	6931	7330 (+6)	1001	1140 (+14)	2824	3193 (+13)
Mexico	62.4	59.1 (−5)	41.6	36.2 (−13)	72.8	77.9 (+7)
Argentina	57.6	80.6 (+40)	19.2	21.7 (+13)	32.8	65.5 (+100)
Venezuela	34.1	15.9 (−53)	17.6	7.3 (−59)	23.1	19.9 (−14)
Colombia	9.4	16.6 (+76)	7.0	20.0 (+186)	3.8	10.7 (+182)
Chile	7.7	14.7 (+91)	8.8	11.2 (+27)	2.5	5.4 (+116)
Brazil	n.a.	85.4 (n.a.)	n.a.	36.2 (n.a.)	n.a.	100.5 (n.a.)

Sources: Country listings in International Advertising Association, *World Advertising Expenditures, 1968* (New York: IAA, 1970), pp. 18, 21, 24; Chile's figures for print and television in 1966, p. 25

Colombia's 1966 figures are from data given in the IAA's *Advertising Investments Around the World* (New York: IAA, 1967), unnumbered pages.

182

TABLE XVI

MEDIA SHARES OF TOTAL PRINT, RADIO, AND TELEVISION ADVERTISING EXPENDITURES, 7 LATIN AMERICAN COUNTRIES AND THE UNITED STATES, 1968

(Percentages to nearest whole number)

	Print	Radio	Television	Combined Electronic Media
Peru	31	20	49	69
Venezuela	37	17	46	63
Brazil	39	16	45	61
Mexico	34	21	45	66
Argentina	48	13	39	52
Colombia	35	42	23	65
Chile	47	36	16	52
United States	63	10	27	37

Source: Calculated from Table XV. Peruvian figures were derived from the same source as those in the table; they applied only to the Lima-Callao region of Peru.

TABLE XVII

DOMESTIC AND OVERSEAS ADVERTISING BILLINGS: TOP TEN U.S. INTERNATIONAL AGENCIES AND SIX OTHERS ACTIVE IN LATIN AMERICA

(Millions of Dollars)

Agency	International billings				Domestic billings			
	1966	1967	1969	1970	1966	1967	1969	1970
J. Walter Thompson	201	227	295	328	380	364	445	436
McCann-Erikson	170	195	158	300	283	281	353	246
Ted Bates & Co.*	88	110	145	160	177	190	230	254
Young & Rubicam	87	104	152	164	320	326	371	356
Ogilvy & Mather	69	69	73	91	98	114	152	159
Foote, Cone & Belding	61	62	63	61	201	207	198	179
Compton	32	55	60	66	105	120	120	120
Norman, Craig & Kummel	41	47	71	86	56	59	69	67
Grant	32	34	42	50	9	8	8	4
Grey	20	30	44	50	154	170	184	201
Kenyon & Eckhart	24	28	12	19	94	85	95	95
Doyle, Dane, Bernbach	20	27	35	41	192	219	235	250
D'Arcy	12	10	—	—	109	111	—	—
Lennen & Newell	10	9	10	20	105	111	116	140
Gardner	5	4	4	5	62	61	54	58
Wells, Rich, Greene	—	1	4	6	10	41	76	91

*Indicates no traceable activity in Latin America.

Source: Advertising Age, February 26, 1968, p. 48 (for top ten), and pp. 31-65, and February 22, 1971, p. 26. Leo Burnett billed $70 million overseas in 1969, $106 million in 1970. Other agencies not reported for 1966-1967 include Benton and Bowles with $40 and $48 million in 1969 and 1970, and SSC&B, which billed $96 million overseas in 1970.

TABLE XVIII

MAJOR U.S. ADVERTISING AGENCIES IN LATIN AMERICA

Agency	Number of countries in which active*		Total billings (millions of dollars)		
	1968	1970	1967	1968	1970[b]
McCann-Erikson	15	16	34.65	41.13	57.44
J. Walter Thompson	6	7	31.00	39.00	60.91
Grant	6	6	10.91	11.41	11.85
Kenyon & Eckhart	5	4	17.32	16.23	4.60
Compton	3	2	8.47	9.89	3.91
Young & Rubicam	2	3	4.81	5.77	10.75
D'Arcy	1	1	6.74	7.43	8.47
Marplan	1	1	—	6.58	10.00
Doyle, Dane, Bernbach	1	1	3.33	5.29	4.42
Grey	1	1	2.50	3.38	5.16
Lennen & Newell	1	1	2.50	2.75	5.05
Foote, Cone & Belding	1	1	2.48	2.52	2.82
Quadrant	1	1	1.50	2.40	2.39
Coordinated Communications	1	n.a.	2.00	1.60	n.a.
Leo Burnett	0	5	.00	.00	13.27
Ogilvy & Mather	0	1(5)[a]	.00	.00	6.70
Benton & Bowles	0	1	.00	.00	3.00
Norman, Craig & Kummel	0	1	.00	.00	2.50

*The reports covered sixteen Latin American countries, all of which have commercial television broadcasting.

[a] Active in five countries in 1970. Billing figure refers to only one.

[b] Includes only billings listed to the agency by name. The number of countries in which active includes partnership arrangements for which there were no billings available.

Source: Compiled from "Eleventh Annual Exclusive Survey of Agencies Operating outside the U.S.", Advertising Age, March 31, 1969 and March 29, 1971.

185

TABLE XIX

OWNERSHIP OF ADVERTISING AGENCIES IN
LATIN AMERICA, BY COUNTRY, 1968 AND 1970*

	Total number of major agencies	Number identified as owned or affiliated with U.S. agency	Number of other foreign agencies	Ownership of largest agency
Argentina	18 (23)	4 (9)	2 (0)	U.S.
Brazil	15 (16)	5 (8)	2 (0)	U.S.
Chile	5 (5)	4 (4)	— (0)	U.S.
Colombia	7 (7)	2 (3)	1 (0)	Domestic
Costa Rica	3 (2)	1 (1)	— (0)	Domestic
Dominican Rep.	2 (3)	2 (3)	— (0)	U.S.
Ecuador	2 (1)	1 (1)	— (0)	U.S.
El Salvador	2 (2)	1 (1)	1 (1)	Mexican
Guatemala	3 (3)	1 (1)	— (0)	Domestic (U.S.)
Honduras	1 (1)	1 (1)	— (0)	U.S.
Mexico	21 (23)	11 (12)	1 (0)	Domestic
Nicaragua	2 (2)	1 (1)	— (0)	Domestic (U.S.)
Panama	5 (4)	2 (2)	— (0)	U.S.
Peru	3 (3)	2 (2)	— (0)	U.S.
Uruguay	3 (3)	1 (2)	— (0)	Domestic (U.S.)
Venezuela	9 (9)	7 (9)	1 (0)	U.S.

*All 1970 figures in parentheses. Largest agency ownership remained unchanged unless otherwise noted.

Sources: The major agencies are those listed in the "Eleventh Annual Exclusive Survey of Agencies Operating outside the U.S.," *Advertising Age*, March 31, 1969, and March 29, 1971. Identification of U.S. and foreign agencies utilized the *Standard Directory of Advertising Agencies.* Since the latter source lists more U.S. agencies than reported in the survey, the confirmed U.S. figures are almost certainly lower than is actually the case.

TABLE XX

U.S. DIRECT INVESTMENT, GROSS NATIONAL PRODUCT, AND TELEVISION AVAILABILITY: EIGHT LATIN AMERICAN COUNTRIES, 1967

	(a) G.N.P. billions of dollar equivalents	(b) Total U.S. direct investment, mill. dollars	(c) U.S. manu- facturing investment (book value, mill. dollars)	(d) Estimated no. of TV receivers in use (thou.)
Brazil	29.7	1326	891	5000
Mexico	24.1	1342	890	2100
Argentina	14.9	1080	677	3200
Venezuela	8.5	2553	310	650
Colombia	5.5	610	192	410
Peru	4.0	605	98	300
Chile	5.4	878	61	300
Panama	0.8	804	33	110

Sources: Column *a* — AID, Gross National Product — Growth Rate and Trend Data, April 25, 1969, p. 8.
Columns *b, c* — AID, Statistics and Reports Division, *Latin America — Economic Growth Trends*, Washington, D.C.: AID, December, 1968, p. 33.
Column *d* — Frappier, *op. cit.*, p. 5.

TABLE XXI

ADVERTISING, MANUFACTURING, AND IMPORTS FROM THE U.S.: FIVE LATIN AMERICAN COUNTRIES (IN MILLIONS OF DOLLARS), 1966

	(1) Total advertising expenditures	(2) Manufacturing component of G.D.P.	(3) Value of imports from the U.S.	(4) U.S. manu- facturing investment (1967)
Mexico	208.0	2740	1026	890
Argentina	180.4	4900	257	677
Venezuela	79.5	1260	614	310
Colombia	27.0	611	324	192
Chile	23.7	1480	269	61

Sources: Column 1 — International Advertising Association, *Advertising Investments Around the World* (New York: IAA, December, 1967).
Column 2 — Computed from Gross Domestic Product and percentage manufacturing data, *UN Statistical Yearbook, 1968*, pp. 568 ff., converted to U.S. dollars.
Columns 3, 4 — AID, Statistics and Reports Division, *Latin America: Economic Growth Trends* (Washington, D.C.: AID, December, 1968), pp. 27 and 33.

TABLE XXII

NET CAPITAL OUTFLOWS TO LESS DEVELOPED COUNTRIES FROM INDUSTRIAL COUNTRIES (AS PERCENTAGE OF THEIR GROSS NATIONAL PRODUCTS) 1961-1968

	1961	1963	1965	1966	1967	1968
16 Industrial countries	.83	.67	.74	.67	.69	.73
France	1.95	1.44	1.25	1.14	1.09	1.16
United Kingdom	1.02	.68	.96	.81	.72	.70
United States	.78	.70	.74	.62	.66	.64
Germany	.84	.50	.57	.57	.86	1.14
Japan	.26	.28	.50	.52	.60	.65
Italy	.45	.38	.41	.83	.33	.64

Source: United Nations, Center for Development Planning, Projections and Policies. (1961 and 1963 figures from the source quoted in *The United Nations and the Business World* [New York: Business International, 1967], p. 3). *The External Financing of Economic Development* (New York: United Nations, 1970), p. 19.

TABLE XXIII

NET INFLOW OF RESOURCES, ELEVEN
LATIN AMERICAN COUNTRIES, 1967 AND 1968

(Millions of Dollars)

	Net receipts of long-term capital and official donations		Net outflow of investment income		Net inflow of new resources	
	1967	1968	1967	1968	1967	1968
Argentina	79	−27	119	142	−40	−169
Bolivia	40	53	18	17	22	36
Brazil	221	241	297	279	−76	−38
Chile	124	278	214	215	−90	63
Colombia	57	180	105	109	−48	71
Ecuador	46	65	25	26	21	39
Mexico	505	543	473	551	32	−8
Paraguay	26	26	5	5	21	21
Peru	168	88	140	142	28	−54
Uruguay	29	29	26	15	4	14
Venezuela	116	218	695	703	−579	−485
23 L.A. countries*	1,848	2,168	2,403	2,520	−555	−352

*Includes Central America, Guyana, Surinan, and the Caribbean.

Source: Center for Development, Projections and Policies, U.N. Department of Economic and Social Affairs. *The External Financing of Economic Development* (New York: United Nations, 1970), p. 91.

Diagrams

Legend List

Diagram 1
Developmental Schema

Diagram 2
Growth Rates and Economic Levels, 51 Non-communist Nations
(Source: *United Nations Statistical Yearbook, 1967)*

Diagram 3
Societal Modes of Development

Diagram 4
Typology of Development Attitude Sets

Diagram 5
Television and Economic Level: 17 Latin American and 20 Developed Countries (Sources: *OECD Observer* [supplement], final statistics for 1967 supplied by Statistics and National Accounts Branch of OECD. Data used for Latin America are tabulated in Table IX.)

Diagram 6
Television Growth in Western Europe and Latin America,* 1955-1967 (Source: USIA, *Overseas Television Developments in 1964,* USIA *Overseas Television Growth in 1965.* The Latin America figure for 1967 is an estimate based on the receiver sets listed in Table IX. It is assumed that the eight countries not listed here but included in USIA computations grew at the same rate.)

191

DIAGRAM 1

DEVELOPMENTAL SCHEMA

Theodorson

Industrialization ⎯⎯⎯⎯⎯⎯⟶ Westernization
(mechanical production (social patterns,
methods) achievements, etc.,
mass consumption)

Kerr

Industrialization ⎯⎯⎯⎯⎯⟶ Open society

Geertz

Economic modernization ⎯⎯⟶ Cultural patterns

Singer

Technology ⎯⎯⎯⎯⎯⟶ Values

Nash

Economic development ⎯⎯⟶ Social structure

Blumer

Industrialization ⎯⎯⎯⟶ Social effects
Society shapes workforce
Industrialization ⎯⟶ Urbanization ⎯⟶ Social effects

Eisenstadt

Modernization (breakdowns possible) subsumes
social, political, and economic development.
Industrialization, rural development, educational changes.

Levy

Modernization (production by power and tools)
⬇ ⬆   ⬇
Centralization,   Economic development
science, specialization,
materialist ethics,
achievement, bureaucratization

192

Bendix

Technological change →Industrialization →Modernization
                       (economic   (social and political
                       changes)   change). Including
                                              education, urbanization,
                                              occupational structure,
                                              democratization, social
                                              mobility, welfare
                                              statism.

Moore

Industrialization ———→ Modernization   (social, political,
(mechanical   and economic changes)
production and   Use of world pool of knowledge, latest
consumption)   methods of organization, health education,
                      welfare, crime, etc.

Apter

West: Commercialization
              ↓ ↑ ———————————→ Modernization (rationalization)
          Industrialization

Non-West:
              Commercialization
                  ↓ ↑ ———————→ Modernization ——→Industrialization
              Bureaucracy

Development
    ↓
Modernization
(control of social consequences of role differentiation)
    ↓
Industrialization

Key to diagram

——————→ causal direction

——————→ two-way or
←—————— mutual causation

——⁄—→ does not cause

193

DIAGRAM 2

**GROWTH RATES AND ECONOMIC LEVELS,
51 NON-COMMUNIST NATIONS**

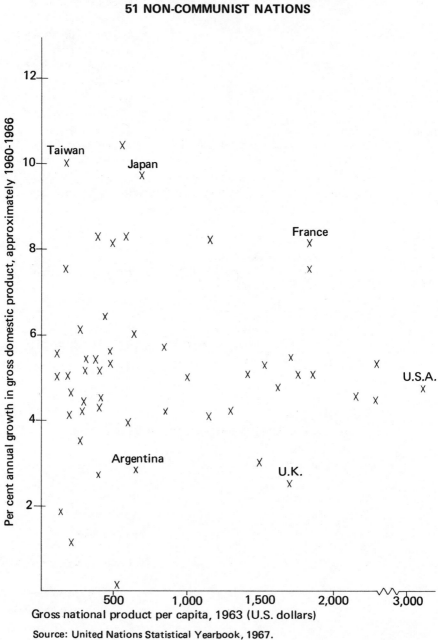

Source: United Nations Statistical Yearbook, 1967.

194

DIAGRAM 3

SOCIETAL MODES OF DEVELOPMENT

Producerism

		High	Low
Consumerism	High	1. Developed or overdeveloped Slow growth	2. Stagnant and declining
	Low	3. Developing	4. Traditional or undeveloped

DIAGRAM 4

TYPOLOGY OF DEVELOPMENT ATTITUDE SETS

Producerism Orientation

		High	Low
Consumerism desires	High	1. Hedonistic	2. Parasitic
	Low	3. Ascetic developmental	4. Traditional

195

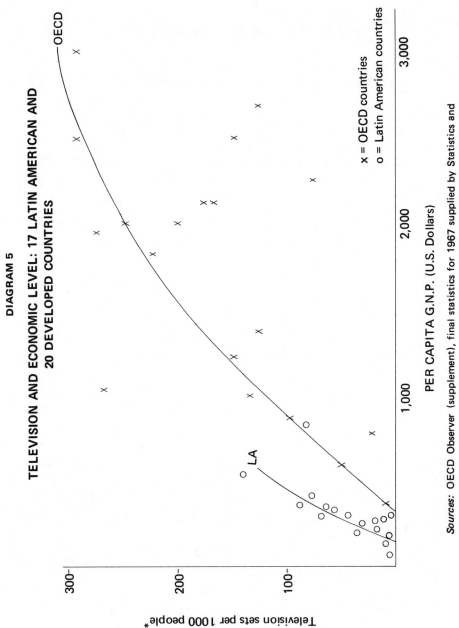

DIAGRAM 5

TELEVISION AND ECONOMIC LEVEL: 17 LATIN AMERICAN AND 20 DEVELOPED COUNTRIES

x = OECD countries
o = Latin American countries

Television sets per 1000 people*

PER CAPITA G.N.P. (U.S. Dollars)

Sources: OECD Observer (supplement), final statistics for 1967 supplied by Statistics and National Accounts Branch of OECD. Data used for Latin America are tabulated in Table IX.

DIAGRAM 6

**TELEVISION GROWTH IN WESTERN EUROPE AND
LATIN AMERICA,* 1955-1967**

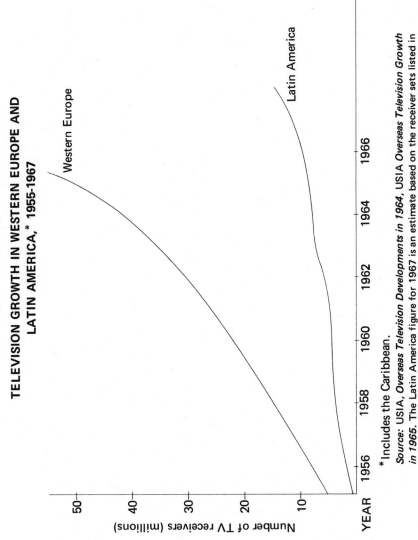

*Includes the Caribbean.

Source: USIA, *Overseas Television Developments in 1964,* USIA *Overseas Television Growth
in 1965. The Latin America figure for 1967 is an estimate based on the receiver sets listed in
Table IX above. It is assumed that the eight countries not listed here but included in USIA
computations grew at the same rate.*

197